COLLEGE ADMISSIONS FOR THE HIGH SCHOOL ATHLETE

College Admissions for the High School Athlete

JACK DISALVO, M.A.
and
THERESA FOY DIGERONIMO, M.Ed

Facts On File

COLLEGE ADMISSIONS FOR THE HIGH SCHOOL ATHLETE

Facts On File, Inc.
460 Park Avenue South
New York NY 10016

Library of Congress Cataloging-in-Publication Data

DiSalvo, Jack.
  College admissions for the high school athlete / Jack DiSalvo and Theresa Foy DiGeronimo.
    p.   cm.
  Includes index.
  ISBN 0-8160-2760-9. — ISBN 0-8160-2816-8 (pbk.)
  1. Universities and colleges—United States—Admission.
  2. College athletes—Recruiting—United States. 3. College applications—United States. I. DiGeronimo, Theresa Foy.
  II. Title.
  LB2351.2.D57   1993
  8.1'056—dc20   93-16811

A British CIP catalogue record for this book is available from the British Library.

Facts On File books are available at special discounts when purchased in bulk quantities for businesses, associations, institutions or sales promotions. Please contact our Special Sales Department in New York at 212/683-2244 or 800/322-8755.

Text design by Grace M. Ferrara
Jacket design by Steve Brower
Composition by Facts On File, Inc.
Manufactured by the Maple-Vail Book Manufacturing Group
Printed in the United States of America

10 9 8 7 6 5 4 3 2 1

This book is printed on acid-free paper.

CONTENTS

ACKNOWLEDGMENTS viii

INTRODUCTION xi

CHAPTER ONE—SETTING REALISTIC AND CONCRETE GOALS 1

  Examining the Good and the Bad 2
  Getting Started Early 3
  Learning to Focus on One Sport 6
  Evaluating Your Skill 8
  Taking the Road Less Traveled 11

CHAPTER TWO—GETTING EXPOSURE 13

  Athletic Camps 14
  Leagues and Tournaments 16
  Choosing the Right Program 17
  Finding the Fine Line 22

CHAPTER THREE—MATCHING ATHLETICS AND ACADEMICS 24

  Selection Guidelines 25
  Five Factors to Consider 27
  Athletic Goals 35
  Matching Schools and Athletes 40

CHAPTER FOUR—CONTACTING COLLEGE COACHES 43
  Your Resume 44
  Timing 51
  Videotapes 53
  Athletic Placement Services 55

CHAPTER FIVE—UNDERSTANDING ATHLETIC RULES AND REGULATIONS 58
  The Purpose of Regulations 59
  Infractions and Penalties 59
  Athletic Associations 62
  Be Smart—Be Safe 75

CHAPTER SIX—TAKING A CAMPUS VISIT 77
  Learning More About the College 78
  Timing Your Visits 79
  Visiting the College Coach 81
  Visiting an Admissions Officer 83
  Visiting a Faculty Member 84
  Visiting a Student-Athlete 85
  Following the Rules 86
  Your Parents and the Interview Process 88
  A Word of Advice 88

CHAPTER SEVEN—COMPILING AN APPLICATION PACKET 90
  Your Best Shot 91
  Sending for the Application Packet 93
  Staying Organized 94
  The Student Section 94
  The Guidance Counselor Section 98
  Teacher Recommendations 99
  From Start to Finish 100
  Timing 102
  The Senior Slide 104

CHAPTER EIGHT—FINDING FINANCIAL AID 108
  The Pros and Cons of Athletic Scholarships 109
  The Facts About Athletic Scholarships 112

NCAA Athletic Scholarships 112
NAIA Athletic Scholarships 117
Admission "Scholarships" 118
Questions to Ask About Athletic Scholarships 119
Other Sources of Financial Aid 120
Compare and Save 124

CHAPTER NINE—MAKING THE FINAL DECISION 127
Selection Criteria 128
The Athletic Program 129
An Unhappy Fit 131
The Final Choice 132
Confirm Your Decision 134
The National Letter of Intent Program 134
Good Luck 137

CHAPTER TEN—FINDING ALTERNATE ROUTES TO
COLLEGE ATHLETICS 138
Two-Year Colleges 139
Prep Schools 144
Walk-ons 146
Club Sports 147
Intramural Athletics 148

APPENDIX—SPORTS ASSOCIATIONS 150
For Specific Sports 150
For General Information 153

INDEX 155

ACKNOWLEDGMENTS

We would like to acknowledge the following people whose input assures that this book is as accurate and up-to-date as possible:

Roberta Anthes, Women's Track Coach, Rutgers University, New Jersey

Jeffrey Cain, College Placement Officer, Admiral Farragut Academy, New Jersey

Angelo Cifaldi, Baseball Coach, Haledon Falcons

Tom DeMaio, Director of Athletics, Hawthorne, High School, New Jersey

Thomas A. DiMicelli, Director of Financial Aid, William Paterson College, New Jersey

Ted Fiore, Head Basketball Coach, St. Peter's College, New Jersey

Sharon Goldbrenner, Field Hockey and Lacrosse Coach, Trenton State College, New Jersey

Lois Gygax, Director of Guidance, DePaul High School, New Jersey

Richard Hilliard, Director of Enforcement, NCAA

Steve Keller, Editor, Middle Atlantic Recruiting Service

Paula Lasalandra, Head Coach, girl's soccer, basketball, softball, DePaul High School, New Jersey

Duane Lindbert, Assistant Commissioner, SW Conference

Arthur Lobbe, New Jersey Basketball Tournament Director, AAU

Shane Lyons, Legislative Assistant, NCAA

Frank McLaughlin, Director of Athletics, Fordham University, New York

Jeffrey H. Orleans, Executive Director, Council of Ivy Group Presidents

Peter Orschiedt, Admissions Officer, Cornell University, New York

Kurt Peterson, Athletic Director, Admiral Farragut Academy, New Jersey

Robert J. Rhoads, Director, Administrative Services, NAIA

Catherine Rice, Communications Director, Women's Sports Foundation

Carl Santaniello, Director of Guidance, Hawthorne High School, New Jersey

Bill Serra, College Athletic Placement Service

Richard Twitchell, Director of Intramurals, Rutgers University, New Jersey

Ron Van Soders, Athletic Director, Rutgers University, New Jersey

Dave Wojcik, Men's Basketball Coach, James Madison University, Virginia

Student Athletes: Bill Burk, Kent Culuko, Chris Hunt, Jennifer Lucia, Al Paz, Lori Toomey

We would also like to thank the many other young athletes who told us their stories and shared their experiences. To ensure their privacy, we have used pseudonyms for all students mentioned in this book. We wish all of you the best of luck.

To my son Matt—an outstanding scholar/athlete

T.D.

To my wife and family for their steady support and encouragement

J.D.

INTRODUCTION

Your athletic skill can open doors to both college admissions and financial aid. Unfortunately for the majority of American high school athletes, wishing and hoping that sports will bring college acceptance and scholarship opportunities won't make it happen—but the practical steps outlined in this book *can* help you realize these goals.

College Admissions for the High School Athlete includes practical and immediately useful information that will explain the ins and outs of sports-propelled college admission. It will teach you how to play the recruiting game and turn the odds to your advantage whether you're a student with a weak academic record who wants to use sports as a stepping stone into higher education, or an exceptional athlete or scholar who'd like to gain admission and a possible scholarship to a selective college. Whatever your goal, through the pages of this book you'll learn how to assess your athletic ability and choose the college, university or junior college that's right for you. You'll get specific instructions on how to gain exposure in your sport and how to make sure college coaches know about you. You'll take an introductory course in the rules and regulations of the athletic associations that govern your recruitment and eligibility. Also, the step-by-step process of requesting and completing college applications and financial aid forms will be discussed as well as the most constructive ways to take a campus visit and make your final decision.

The recruiting process is basically the same for all athletes. So this book presents its information without separating the facts for male and female athletes—the rules of the game are the same for both. The recruiting process is also the same in all sports most commonly played in college. These include: baseball, basketball, cross country, fencing, field hockey, football, golf, gymnastics, ice hockey, lacrosse, soccer, softball, swimming and diving, track, tennis, volleyball and wrestling.

Whatever your sport, whatever your reasons for wanting to compete on a college team, *College Admissions for the High School Athlete* will give you the information you need to ensure that if you have athletic skill and you want to go to college and compete on an intercollegiate team, you can.

Although both authors have worked closely together to prepare and write this book, the first person voice that speaks to the reader is that of Jack DiSalvo.

*　*　*

The information in this book is presented as a reference guide. Although at the time of publication, all facts have been verified as accurate and up-to-date, changes do occur so be sure to check with the college office of admissions or the athletic department for their specific recruiting and admissions requirements.

C H A P T E R 1

SETTING REALISTIC AND CONCRETE GOALS

In the spring of his senior year, Dave Winfield was offered a partial scholarship to play baseball at the University of Minnesota. At the same time he was drafted by the Baltimore Orioles to play in the minors. In his book, *Winfield: A Player's Life* (W.W. Norton, 1988), Winfield recalls, "A lot of my friends thought the choice was obvious. One or two years in the minors and I could be in the big leagues. A half scholarship to the 'U' meant living at home for four years, having to go to all those classes, and just scraping by." But Dave had set precise goals for himself *before* the recruiters came knocking on his high school door. Because Dave Winfield's first priority at that time was to get an education, he surprised his friends, took the scholarship offer and headed off to college.

This chapter will help you gain the same clear sense of direction so you can set concrete and realistic goals that will carry you into intercollegiate sports.

EXAMINING THE GOOD AND THE BAD

Although you probably don't have to choose between college ball and a professional contract like Dave Winfield, you will have to make some difficult decisions. To do this successfully you need to know both the good and the bad about college athletics before you run blindly toward a gilded dream. Most athletes know all about the good side of college sports. Through intercollegiate programs athletes can continue to participate in the sport they love at a more challenging level of competition; they can often use their skill to gain admission to schools that otherwise would be out of their reach. And the better athletes can even use their sport to pay the cost of higher education. Once enrolled in college, student-athletes frequently become privileged members of the student body. They often don't have to stand on line like everyone else to schedule their classes; they can sometimes side-step attendance requirements, they are fed non-cafeteria-type food, and many are offered personal tutoring. However, there is another side to college athletics.

The privileges don't come free. A great deal of responsibility and pressure accompanies the athletic route through college. Athletes give back to the school inordinate amounts of time in practice, competitive events and traveling throughout the season; they owe coaches an all-out effort and consistently top-level performances, and all the time the athlete is expected to adjust to college life and achieve academic success. Unfortunately, some students aren't prepared to handle the pressure of collegiate athletics and academics; many fail their courses, quit school or give up athletics completely.

A football star from a neighboring high school is a good example of an athlete who wasn't ready for the down side of college athletics. This young man won numerous division and state titles in his junior and senior years of high school. He was heavily recruited by college coaches and was flattered to think that the sport he worked so hard to master was finally going to pay off and help him reach his goal of becoming a doctor. He chose the scholarship offer of a prestigious and selective university 200 miles from his home. At the end of his first semester he quit, headed back home and is now commuting to a nearby state college. This player's football coach feels that the young man simply couldn't find a way to put in the time on the field and earn the grades he needed to enter medical school. His goals clashed and one of them had to go. "I thought college ball would be like high school ball," the player admits. "I never had trouble before balancing my school time and football time, but in college it's just not the same. The expectations are higher; the time commitment is unbelievable, and I was always putting football ahead of my studies. It just didn't work for me."

Of course not all college athletes buckle under the pressure, but if you're considering college sports you should know that the pressure exists. As I'll explain later in the book, you should find out about both sides of college athletics by talking with college players. You should spend time with the team when you visit a campus. You should carefully assess and match your athletic and academic talents. Then if you choose to try for a spot on a college team, you can, without reservation, pursue it with the same determination and planning you instinctively know pay off in any competitive arena.

GETTING STARTED EARLY

Athletes who plan to use their athletic skills to gain college admission need to set goals—and the sooner the better. There are, of course, stories that illustrate the exception to the rule, but generally the students who have the best chance of navigating unscathed through the college recruiting and selection process are the ones who know two things early in their high school years: (1) they want to go to college, and (2) they want to participate in a sport on the college level.

Making the Grade

The sooner you set college as your first goal, the sooner you can begin the task of keeping your grades up to admission-level standards. Admissions officers are not impressed with eleventh hour efforts that show a senior student has the ability to perform academically; instead they see only that this capable student chose not to perform for the three years prior and now doesn't meet admission requirements. The bane of college recruiters is the all-too-common scenario of baiting and finally hooking talented high school athletes only to have to let them go because they don't meet academic eligibility requirements.

Both the National Collegiate Athletic Association (NCAA) and the National Athletic Intercollegiate Association (NAIA) (the governing bodies who set the eligibility rules for almost all four-year athletic programs) have set academic eligibility requirements. Athletes who want to practice or play in their freshman year at schools in either athletic association must attain the established minimum grade-point average and SAT or ACT score. (See Chapter Five for a complete list of these requirements.) In both the NCAA and the NAIA, student-athletes who meet the admission standards must continue to meet established academic requirements throughout their college years to remain eligible to compete. These rules aren't flexible—even for highly recruited, blue-chip athletes.

Just ask basketball player Tom Simon of Paterson, New Jersey. In 1991 Simon was a top choice among the nation's college basketball recruiters. His playing talent led news reporters to tout him as the best player to ever come out of this basketball-driven inner city. But when Simon couldn't come up with the necessary 700 SAT score, the offers from powerhouses like Georgetown, Villanova and North Carolina State were withdrawn. Once the word was out about Simon's weak academic record, the letters stopped coming; his phone stopped ringing and the recruiters moved on to other players who could make the grade. Today, Tom Simon is playing without a scholarship or fame at a two-year community school. He may work his way back up, but his experience should make it clear that before young athletes immerse themselves in their sport, they should know, first and foremost, that what happens in the classroom during the four years of high school is directly related to intercollegiate athletic opportunities.

Planning Ahead

If intercollegiate athletics is your goal, setting that goal early will enable you to pursue it aggressively, thoroughly and successfully. This philosophy is no different than the academic one that guides college-bound students from their freshman through senior year.

Students who know when they enter high school that they want to go to college are scheduled by their guidance counselors in college-required courses. These students may even take elective courses and participate in extracurricular activities that improve their admissions potential in specific fields of study. For example, students who intend to major in nursing follow a college-prep curriculum and often choose science-oriented courses. Many join future nurses clubs and volunteer at local hospitals. When senior year comes around, these students have everything they need to pursue their goal. But other students who decide only in their senior year to go to college and major in nursing may find that their high school academic record and course selections do not satisfy admissions requirements. If they do, the lack of planning may put them at a disadvantage when competing for college admission with better prepared and focused applicants.

The same forethought and preparation that so obviously enhances college admission possibilities also enhances your chances of being recruited by the schools of your choice. Year after year I watch the athletes who were focused and determined throughout high school achieve their goals more readily than those who strive to attain the same goals in their senior year.

For example, when senior shooting guard Joe Feeney began making headlines as his basketball team's high scorer he decided to try to get a basketball scholarship. Although his coach quickly sent out letters of interest to the colleges Joe hoped to play for, in the recruiting process Joe was at a disadvantage to other high school players who had planned ahead. Paul Walker, for example, was a player in Joe's league who had made the decision in his sophomore year to try for a college team. During his sophomore and junior years Paul attended numerous clinics to improve his technique; he spent two summers playing on Amateur Athletic Union (AAU) teams where he was observed by scouts, recruiters and sports reporters, and he worked with coaches in his school and in clinics who helped him critically and honestly evaluate his potential. In the summer before his senior year Paul and his coach sent letters of interest to the colleges Paul wanted to attend. Now Paul is an active competitor in the recruiting game, but Joe's haphazard and late entry will make it more difficult (although not impossible) for him to win a spot on a college team.

This doesn't mean that senior-year athletes can't decide to play a college sport and succeed in doing so. Just as some senior students can suddenly decide they do want to go to college and successfully scramble to meet admission requirements, senior-year athletes can do the same in intercollegiate sports. Last-minute decisions do mean, however, that the athlete will need to hustle through the recruiting process and may lose opportunities in the more selective schools. If you have gotten a late start in the recruiting game but are now determined to make a college team, the information in this book will be especially helpful to you—you don't have time to make a mistake. Gather together knowledge about the recruiting process and then go after what you want.

LEARNING TO FOCUS ON ONE SPORT

When athletes make the decision to pursue intercollegiate athletics early, they often can improve their recruiting potential by concentrating on *one* sport only. All-American, multisport athletes are usually well-rounded individuals who enjoy year-round competition and a variety of physical challenges. But for the majority of high school athletes this versatility takes away the time and concentration needed to develop fully the proficiency level necessary for intercollegiate competition.

Focusing is another area in which early goal setting is helpful. Freshman and sophomore students who decide to reach for college athletics have the opportunity to pick and choose the sports that, based on their skill and the colleges' needs, have the greatest potential for opening college doors and/or offering scholarships. A softball player, for example, might choose to switch to lacrosse if her softball team is full of superstars or if she feels colleges are more in need of lacrosse players. Likewise, a so-so basketball player might choose to switch to wrestling where he'll get more competitive time and increase his chances of compiling an impressive record.

An early decision to focus on one sport also allows athletes to make constructive use of off-season time. As explained in Chapter Two, playing in non-high school leagues and tournaments and attending off-season camps greatly improves recruiting potential because this sharpens skills and offers exposure to college coaches. This time can also be used to develop greater muscle strength through weight training. In the past decade weight training has become a necessary part of sport-training programs. Experts once believed that strength training was counterproductive for athletes. They feared that additional muscle mass would make the athlete "muscle-bound" and therefore reduce flexibility, speed and ease of motion. Recent research has found, however, that just the opposite is true: proper strength training improves muscular strength and can actually increase flexibility, enhance speed and add to the fluidity and range of body movement. These factors not only make athletes more competitive, they reduce the risk of injury and injury recovery time—both valuable assets to athletes *and* college coaches. When first evaluating the recruitability of a high school athlete, colleges coaches frequently want to know, "Is he on a weight-training program?" Or, "How often does she work out?"

Female athletes, too, should be actively involved in strength training. Because women don't produce the male hormone testosterone, they can't (and shouldn't aim to) develop bulging muscles, but they can and should use a supervised program to tone, firm and strengthen their muscles to gain the competitive advantage.

There are, as always, some exceptions to the rule that says high school athletes should focus on one sport only. Football players, for example, can't easily practice their game year round; some wisely use spring track to improve their speed and agility. Many field hockey players enhance their game by also participating in lacrosse. (It's not unheard of for these girls to get partial scholarships in both!) So, I'm not saying that multisport athletes can't play on the college level—a great many do. I am saying, however, that in most cases the skilled, one-sport athlete has the recruiting advantage.

When choosing one sport on which to hang hopes of college admission or when simply wondering if a chosen sport can open college doors, you should consider these two things: (1) personal skill, and (2) the colleges' needs.

EVALUATING YOUR SKILL

Before you enter your senior-year season, you need an objective assessment of your ability and potential. This is a crucial but sensitive and often overlooked point. Parents are notoriously biased judges, so in all fairness you should disqualify them from evaluating your athletic capabilities. Guidance counselors, too, although invaluable in assessing academic potential and skill, are most often unable to advise students on whether or not their athletic skills are college material. This leaves your coach as the first most valuable resource for athletic skill evaluation.

Unfortunately, too often athletes wait for the coach to notice exceptional skill and approach them about the possibility of competing in college. Goal setting, however, isn't the coach's responsibility—it's yours. Once you decide that you might want to use athletics as an avenue to college, you have to tell your coach. This news is nothing to hide or feel bashful about. Just as you wouldn't hesitate to ask a guidance counselor to give an objective evaluation of your academic record and chances of being accepted into college, don't hesitiate to ask your coach to work with you toward your goal of college admission through high school sports.

Early in the athletic season (preferably no later than the junior year) arrange for a private meeting with your coach. (As you wouldn't ask a teacher to rate your ability in front of other students, don't put a coach on the spot in front of the team.) Explain your goal and ask the coach to help decide if it is a realistic one. Some coaches will feel confident giving an immediate opinion; others will need more time to observe, compile statistics and gather information. When the coach does respond, be prepared for the good and the bad with a simple "Why?" response.

To better understand how a coach can explain his or her reasons for encouraging or discouraging a student to pursue college sports, consider this situation, which a fellow coach recently faced with members of her softball team. Two players, I'll call them Jane and Wendy, both expressed an interest in playing college softball. Jane's parents weren't sure their daughter could go to a good four-year college because her combined SAT score was only 795. The coach had no qualms assuring Jane and her parents that if Jane kept up her classroom grades and continued playing softball she would surely be accepted at some good, fairly selective schools. Why? Because the coach knew that on the pitching mound Jane had the body size, experience and game statistics to earn her a slot on a number of college teams (and therefore in the classroom). At 5'9" and 140 pounds, Jane had been clocked pitching 87 mph and had earned double-digit strikeouts in every game that year. She had attended winter clinics at a local college, had been playing summer ball for three years and had even given up tennis to play in a fall softball league. That's why in her junior year the coach could, with very specific reasons, confidently encourage Jane and her family to pursue college softball opportunities.

Wendy also wanted to play college ball and more fortunately than her friend had earned exceptionally high SAT scores. However, the coach felt she would be misleading Wendy if she encouraged her to pursue college-level play. Why? Because relative to other high school players, Wendy was quite average. She played a terrific third base; the coach could count on her to stay mentally alert and grab line drives and ground balls and throw them to first base on target, but she had a weak bat, a frail body build, unimpressive statistics and until this point only a seasonal interest in softball. With enough recruiting effort and determination, Wendy could probably play in a small college or a two-year community college, but with her outstanding academic record these kinds of schools were not in the game plan. As much as Wendy enjoyed playing softball, was an asset to the team and was in need of scholarship money, the coach had to discourage her from setting college softball as a goal.

This coach gave both Jane and Wendy very specific reasons for their skill evaluation. When you ask a coach to assess your ability, don't settle for a quick, "Oh, absolutely, you can go to any college you want on an athletic scholarship." Or, "You gotta be dreaming. Forget it." Ask "Why?" Then get a second opinion.

Get a Second Opinion

Wendy and her family took the coach's advice and did not try to sell Wendy's skills to college recruiters. But what if they didn't think the coach was right? If you disagree with a coach's evaluation of your skill level, or if you have any doubts about the coach's ability to realistically evaluate skill level, you certainly should look for a second opinion. In fact, just as you might want a second medical opinion before agreeing to surgery even when you have faith in your own doctor's abilities, it's a good idea in almost any circumstance to look for another evaluation.

Asking another coach to take a look at an athlete in action is the quickest and easiest way to get back-up assessment. Without arguing with the primary coach or even implying that you don't trust his or her judgment, you can simply ask for help in getting another evaluation from a coach from another school system. Most coaches will not take this request as an insult; they are on friendly terms with many other coaches and can easily arrange to have one of them visit your school or even watch as you play their team as rivals. Coaches know that college sports recruiting demands a great deal of time and effort from an athlete and yet offers enticing rewards, so it's certainly logical for you to want to double-check your chances before giving up or venturing out at full speed.

If you don't feel comfortable telling the primary coach that you want a second opinion, there are other ways to get one. You can ask for assistance from the coach at a local college. Call and explain that you are considering participating in college athletics but you're not sure if you have the talent to realistically set such a goal. Then ask if anyone from the college's athletic department could possibly observe an upcoming competition and give you an informal evaluation. If this can't be arranged, ask if you might send a videotape of a competition for a cursory assessment. College coaches are always looking down the road for talent; yours would not be an un-welcomed or unusual request. (At NCAA Division I and II schools you'll have to wait until after your junior year to ask for this feedback from college coaches.)

You can also get objective feedback from several other impartial sources. As I will explain in detail in Chapter Two, many student athletes enhance their skill level at off-season clinics and camps. Here, instructors are quite capable of sizing up an athlete's college potential relative to other athletes in that sport. Also, there are professional scouts and placement counselors who, for a fee, will let you know if you're of college caliber. (Before you look for this kind of input, however, be sure to read Chapter Two; not all commercial programs will be right for you.)

Objective skill evaluation is often the toughest part of early goal setting. But don't put it off. If you have what it takes, it's worth the effort to try to make a college team. But if the talent just isn't there, it's best to know that too so you don't waste valuable time and effort chasing an unrealistic goal.

TAKING THE ROAD LESS TRAVELED

As you set your college goals, you should consider the full range of college athletic opportunities available—not just the ones you see on TV. Recruiting in football and in men's and women's basketball (and baseball to a lesser degree), for example, is intensely competitive. Obviously, in pure numbers there are many more athletes playing these sports than any other high school sport and so the chances of being selected by a college coach are automatically diminished. But also, in many four-year colleges and universities these sports are revenue-producing activities. Many recruiters and coaches put their jobs on the line every time they sign a new player. Media interest is keen in these sports, so a losing season can negatively affect the college's public image; stadiums, financed by the college, fill to capacity only when the teams are winning, and alumni donations inevitably rise and fall in direct relation to the team's successes and failures.

If you are the star of your high school football, basketball or baseball team and you love the game, you'll surely want to buck the odds and give college recruiting in these sports your best shot. But for those of you who don't excel in or enjoy these sports there are many other athletic activities that can open college doors and pay the bill as well. In fact, athletes who are in the position of having to drop one sport to concentrate fully on another, or who are looking for one sport that will carry them into intercollegiate competition should certainly consider taking a road less traveled.

A quick count through the men's and women's National Directory of College Athletics lists these 17 other intercollegiate sports:

crew	ice hockey	swimming
cross country	lacrosse	tennis
fencing	polo	track and field
field hockey	skiing	volleyball
golf	soccer	wrestling
gymnastics	squash	

A few colleges also recruit and aid athletes proficient in rodeo, badminton, frisbee or parachuting. Obviously, for determined male and female athletes, there are plenty of opportunities to participate in intercollegiate sports. Your job is to learn how to go after the opportunities and land in a place that is well matched to both your athletic and academic capabilities. The rest of the chapters in this book will help you make that perfect match.

CHAPTER 2

GETTING EXPOSURE

The summer before seventh grade Ken Carlson went to camp. It wasn't the kind of camp you might remember where kids spend their days fishing, swimming and hiking. At 12 years of age, Ken was already preparing to use the sport he loved to buy himself a quality education—he went to basketball camp. Ken attended Five-Star and AAU camps and played on inner-city leagues throughout high school. Now he says, "I don't care if you get your name in headlines everyday; if you're from a small town like mine you have to get out and get your name known by playing at all-star camps and in leagues that give you top-level competition."

For Ken the plan worked. After playing in the Eastern Invitational Tournament the summer after his junior year, Ken found himself smack in the middle of the recruiting frenzy. Finally, after sitting down with coaches from seven different schools and visiting five campuses, Ken accepted a full scholarship to Division I James Madison University in Virginia. He signed his Letter of Intent in

October—a full month before his senior year basketball season even began.

Carlson's story is not an exceptional one. In the college recruiting arena, exposure beyond the interscholastic team has become a necessary prerequisite. Except in some major metropolitan high schools that have drawing power and in the sport of football, which uses films to attract recruiters, most athletes aren't discovered on their home turf; they have to go where the college coaches, recruiters and scouts are bound to be—at noninterscholastic camps, leagues and tournaments. As with every step of the college recruiting process, carefully planned exposure opportunities can be quite successful, but haphazard or misdirected ones are frustrating and futile. This chapter will help you make sure that if you venture out for exposure the experience will be productive.

ATHLETIC CAMPS

As the Ken Carlsons of high school sports know, summer is no longer the time for pick-up games on the playground. It's time to head out to athletic camps. If you seriously want to pursue college-level competition, summer camps are one way of getting known and building a reputation among college coaches. But before you pack your bags, do a groundwork investigation to be sure the camp will meet your goals.

The word *camp* can mean a lot of different things. Day camps (often called commuter camps) attract local kids and are usually staffed by local high school and/or college coaches. These camps generally run three to five days and cost between $40 and $100. If one of these camps is run by coaches from a college you hope to attend, then that's the place to go. But otherwise, commuter camps do not usually offer the exposure found at overnight camps.

Overnight camps seem to have become the summer homes of many college recruiters. These camps are usually held on college campuses, they run for five to six days, the athletes are housed in dormitories and the cost can run up to $500. There are, however, some major differences you should consider when choosing an overnight camp. Some are primarily instructional. They are staffed by experienced athletes and coaches and they focus on physical conditioning, skill-related workouts, educational films, lectures and academic counseling. Others are simply showcases. They do little more than put kids together to compete before college coaches, recruiters and scouts.

Both instructional and showcase camps have their advantages and disadvantages. Instructional camps are the most worthwhile for younger athletes who are still perfecting skills. But they don't attract many recruiters and junior- and senior-year athletes may find the clinic-type atmosphere boring. Showcase camps offer more opportunities to compete and show off, which can help you build a reputation and judge your capabilities against the barometer of other athletes who also hope to compete on the college level.

When choosing a showcase camp: Beware. Many of the biggest and most publicized camps recruit the nation's top high school athletes in the hope of attracting more college recruiters. Then they fill the majority of slots with less talented campers who pay top price to be overshadowed by the superstars. It's not that the less talented athletes don't have the ability to compete in college; it's just that, because the competitions at camps are often quick and unstructured, the recruiters are distracted by the big name participants.

A recent article in *Sports Illustrated* ("The Summer Game," July 15, 1991) described at length how this problem is especially present at basketball camps. Traditional big-name boy's camps like Garfinkel's Five-Star camps in Pennsylvania and Virginia, Cronauer's B/C All-Stars camps in Georgia and Krider's All-American camps in Ohio now compete with camps sponsored by commercial names like Nike and LA Gear. Camp promoters may spend hundreds of thousands of dollars each summer to fund basketball camps that lure the best players with offers of free equipment, all-expenses-paid trips and all-around royal treatment. Then they charge hefty fees to the hundreds of other players who fill in the gaps but soon find themselves worn down, discouraged and overlooked.

When choosing an athletic camp you can't assume it's a legitimate, productive enterprise. The athletic summer camp business is the most unregulated aspect of high school and college athletics. George Raveling, chairman of the NCAA recruiting committee, is quoted in *Sports Illustrated* as saying, "The high school federations have no control because school isn't in session and the NCAA is reluctant to get involved because we're talking about kids who aren't in college. It's no wonder you see increasing abuses take place." If Raveling has his way the NCAA will soon find itself in the summer camp business, and it will dictate that Division I coaches be allowed to attend only NCAA camps. The NCAA will hold the sponsoring college or university responsible for any breach of regulations. Until then, you'll need to establish your own evaluation criteria and find a camp where you can get the dual experience of competing with college level athletes *and* having the opportunity to be evaluated fairly by college coaches. (See pages 19–22 for a discussion of camp evaluation criteria.)

LEAGUES AND TOURNAMENTS

If you can't afford or choose not to go to summer camps, you can still gain exposure by competing in noninterscholastic leagues and tournaments. This is a good move especially if you compete in weak or little-known conferences. There are many opportunities, especially during the off-season, to compete in leagues and tournaments that offer better competition, that push you to excel beyond your high school level and that give you a realistic view of your skills.

Off-season leagues and tournaments can also help you focus on your sport. As I explained in Chapter One, it's helpful for high school athletes to chose one sport and concentrate on becoming the best in that one area. Off-season leagues keep athletes in shape, give them opportunities to practice and put them in places where they can build their reputation.

There are many well-established programs that offer serious athletes the opportunity to expand their competitive environment. A local sophomore tennis player, for example, has joined the U.S. Tennis Association; she practices year-round and competes in six sectional tournaments each year. This player has earned a respectable ranking in the USTA and hopes to qualify for the national tournament next year. Also, several of our basketball players play in summer leagues sponsored by the Amateur Athletic Union (AAU). This year, in fact, a local AAU team, the Jayhawks, has compiled such an impressive record it's going to the LA Gear/BCI (Basketball Congress International) Invitational Tournament at Arizona State where they'll compete against the best players in the country. Some of my own baseball players compete in the summer American Legion league and the fall regional league. These off-season teams (like the Stan Musial, Connie Mack and Babe Ruth teams) play full schedules and have county and state championship games that will give players many opportunities to show off their stuff for scouts and recruiters (many of whom seem to be more available in the off-season).

There are similar exposure opportunities in wrestling, volleyball, field hockey, swimming, lacrosse, soccer and almost every other athletic activity. Although similar in opportunity, keep in mind that most leagues and tournaments vary in structure. Some leagues require athletes to try out for a spot on the team; others make room for anyone who is interested. Some tournaments are played by invitation only; others run on elimination championship schedules, and still others are open only to athletes highly ranked by the sponsoring organizations. The cost too is variable: Some cost the athlete nothing; others require a registration, entrance or membership fee. Some are relatively inexpensive but if held out-of-state become quite costly. In 1991, for example, parents and sponsors from Portland, Oregon, collected $7,000 to send their youth basketball team (age 14 and under) to the national AAU tournament in Virginia. The tournament itself cost the team only $550; the rest was needed to pay for transportation, room and board.

CHOOSING THE RIGHT PROGRAM

Because camps, leagues and tournaments can be quite different in format, eligibility requirements, cost and exposure opportunities you should take some time to locate and evaluate the programs that are best for you.

Locate

The most valuable resource for locating good camps, leagues and tournaments should be your high school coach. All coaches receive piles of letters, flyers, postcards and brochures advertising these kinds of athletic programs. Many coaches have personal experience with noninterscholastic competitions and can guide you to the ones most appropriate to your level of ability. It's also the high school coach who can enter your team in tournaments and leagues outside the interscholastic schedule. Ask your coach if your team can compete in any of these events.

Another source of information is the college coach. There's no reason you shouldn't call coaches at the colleges you might like to attend, explain that you're looking for quality athletic programs, and ask for suggestions. Most coaches will be willing to give not only this information, but will also suggest where in your area you're most likely to be observed by recruiters and scouts.

Finally, a sound source of information is the national or regional association affiliated with your sport. In the appendix, you'll find a list of 21 sport associations. Each one offers referrals to camps, clinics, leagues and tournaments and many sponsor their own athletic events. The Lacrosse Federation, for example, keeps a record of various clinics and camps and publishes a magazine in which male and female athletic programs are listed; there is even a special designation made for camps that are primarily showcases. In the same way, young tennis players who join the USTA by paying a $10.00 membership fee automatically receive a camp directory and lists of tournament locations and schedules. Another source of information is the Amateur Athletic Union, which sponsors clinics, camps, leagues and tournaments in most male and female sports. If you call the national headquarters number listed in the appendix, a representative will give you the name and number of your regional director. Sport associations are established to encourage participation and enjoyment of athletics; call them to find out what referral and resource information they can make available to you.

Once you've collected the names, locations and schedules of a number of athletic activities, you'll need to evaluate them before you choose the ones you'll attend.

Evaluate

You should expect to gain three things from noninterscholastic sports programs: (1) exposure, (2) experience and (3) skill improvement. So before you sign up for any camp, clinic, league or tournament you should get on the phone and find out exactly what the program offers.

CONSIDER LEVEL OF COMPETITION

Investigate the caliber of athletes who are involved in the program. Do athletes try out for a spot so that only the better athletes participate? Is it invitational so that only the best athletes participate? Or, is it open to anyone so that the level will span from so-so to very talented?

Level of competition is an important factor in the evaluation process. It's counterproductive for you to spend time and effort working out with or competing against athletes consistently below your own level. But it's also risky to jump into a level too far over your head. As mentioned earlier, the talented athlete who struggles to keep up with the blue-chippers can not only lose confidence but also lose positive recruiting opportunities. Going to "The Best" camp or tournament is not always the best choice. You should seek your own level and play where the competition is challenging but fair.

The exact level of any athletic event is difficult to assess but you should make an effort to get a general idea before you sign up. Ask program organizers to define the level of competition at their events and ask for the phone numbers of athletes who have participated in the program in the past. Most young athletes are quite willing to share their experiences and may in the end be your best source for an honest appraisal. Finally, if you have the time and opportunity to observe the program at an earlier session, this too will give you insight into the participants' competitive level.

CONSIDER EXPOSURE POTENTIAL

Nonscholastic athletic programs can be fun and educational but once you set intercollegiate competition as your ultimate goal, the who-will-see-me factor becomes a major consideration when choosing one program over another. Because some activities are geared primarily toward instruction and others toward exposure, when you inquire about a program, ask which one you can expect. Be very direct in getting this information by asking program organizers for specific details: "Do college coaches attend your program for the purpose of recruiting?" "What colleges sent representatives last year?" "Who do you expect will be there this year?"

If you have already selected some colleges you'd like to attend, you have two other avenues to help you consider exposure potential. One: Call the coaches at these schools, explain that you are looking for a camp, league or tournament for off-season competition and ask the coaches to recommend some that are likely to be scouted by their recruiters.

If none of the recommended programs are in your area or price range, then take the second approach: Ask the coaches which recruiting services they subscribe to. Recruiting services send coaches scouting reports from many events and locations that the college recruiters themselves can not possibly attend. These reports usually list names of talented athletes accompanied by personal information such as age, height, weight, school and year of graduation; they often give each athlete a rating number that correlates to the collegiate level the scout feels the athlete can compete on. This information helps coaches find the talent they're looking for. Get the phone number of the services from the college coaches; call them and ask, "Where will you be scouting this summer?" Be sure to tell the scouts that because the college you'd like to attend buys their recruiting service, when you choose a camp, league, or tournament you'd like it to be one that the service will be covering. Also, when you know you're competing in certain leagues or tournaments, send that information to the recruiting services and try to persuade them to scout the program. If the competition level is high enough and there will be a number of recruitable athletes in attendance, the scouts for commercial services can often be persuaded to include the event in their schedules.

If competing on the college level is your goal, it's foolish to spend time, money and sweat on athletic programs that nobody knows about. When choosing non-interscholastic sports activities be sure to calculate exposure potential into your decision-making formula.

CONSIDER COST

Exposure can be the most expensive factor in the college recruiting process, so it certainly needs to be considered when evaluating athletic programs. The answer to the question, "What is the cost of exposure?" depends on your goals. If you expect to attend a local Division III state college, it's not necessary to spend thousands of dollars to go camp and tournament hopping around the country. Local college coaches are likely to attend high school events if they're notified that an athlete is interested in being recruited; they are also more likely to attend area off-season events where local athletes can be evaluated without spending a fortune. On the other hand, if you hope to get a full scholarship to a highly competitive Division I college you may decide, for example, that a $3,000 investment in athletic programs across the country may be worth the return in scholarships valued at $80,000. If you talk to athletes who have spent the money and won scholarships, you'll hear that the programs are worth every penny. If you talk to those who have spent large sums on exposure opportunities and didn't land lucrative scholarships, they'll tell you it's a waste of money. That's why the bottom line on putting down big bucks on noninterscholastic athletic events is that it's a gamble. If you spend the money now on top-notch programs you might get it back (and more) in scholarship dollars, but then again you might not.

When deciding how much you'll pay for exposure don't be fooled by an impressive price tag. Too often we assume that the higher the cost the better the program, but that's a debatable point when it comes to athletic camps. It's difficult to say that cost is an indicator of quality because quality is relative to how well the program fits your needs—not how well-known it is or how well its brochure is written.

The decision to spend money on exposure should be made with an objective eye to your potential. As recommended in Chapter One, be sure to get a thorough and objective evaluation of your skill and then decide how much you want to spend to spread the word.

FINDING THE FINE LINE

Let's suppose for a moment that skill and cost aren't an issue—you have the talent and the money. How much exposure is necessary? The answer is hard to pinpoint and worrisome to many coaches, recruiters and program organizers. As showcase events become more popular, top athletes are afraid to miss any opportunity to be seen in action. So they drag themselves from one event to another, losing a bit more interest, strength and spirit with each stop. Bob Gibbons, recruiter for the Nike basketball camps, has told *Sports Illustrated*, "They play too many games, attend too many camps, and spread themselves too thin."

Steve Keller, Division I basketball scout and editor of the *MidAtlantic Sporting News*, is also concerned. "I've seen kids," he says, "who attend four different basketball camps in the month of July alone. They don't realize that this kills their intensity and edge. The college coaches walk in to watch and they see the kid looking flat. They look at me and say, 'This kid doesn't have enough speed to play for us.' Well I know that they're not really seeing what the kid can do. They should come back and see him again after he's had a chance to rest for a few days and isn't so worn down." But Keller and the kids know—the coaches won't be back.

To find the fine line between going unnoticed and going overboard, Keller suggests that you choose to participate in only a few quality athletic events. By quality he means events that are scheduled when you are (1) healthy, (2) ready to play, (3) have your mind in it and (4) are playing with the right people in the right setting.

These circumstances can promote quality performances but your best performances won't happen if you choose athletic programs haphazardly or focus too intently on mere quantity. Use the information in this chapter to select the opportunities that will be most beneficial to you in terms of exposure, experience and improvement but that won't apply too much pressure, take up all your free time or make you feel like you're selling your youth for a free ride to college.

MATCHING ATHLETICS AND ACADEMICS

In his small-town high school young Larry Bird was a highly recruited basketball player. Among many others, Purdue, Louisville, Indiana State and Indiana University wanted him. Bird remembers that his dad liked them all; no matter which college was mentioned he'd say, "Good place, Larry, good place." Everybody else—his coach, his mother and his friends—wanted him to go to Indiana University. And so he did. In his book, *Drive: The Story of My Life* (Doubleday, 1989), Bird says, "They made the decision for me. In a way I just went along with what they felt was best for me." But "everybody else" didn't have to live at the school or earn a degree there. It didn't take Bird long to realize that he and Indiana University were mismatched. Even before basketball practice began on October 15 he packed his bag and headed home. Looking back now he feels that although he had gotten good enough grades in high school, "I wasn't ready for a school the size of Indiana

University. I was intimidated by the size of it and it got so I just couldn't handle it."

Everyone knew that Bird could play ball at this school but everyone forgot that athletics is not all that college is about. Like Larry Bird, many young students follow athletic dreams that lead them to institutions that aren't right for them. Because there are approximately 2,500 colleges in this country, it's not surprising that finding one that's "just right" is a difficult job—especially for student-athletes. You must not only find a college or university that matches your academic level, needs and goals, you have the additional responsibility of finding one that fits your athletic abilities and goals as well. Many high school athletes run off with fingers crossed to the college that offers them the best scholarship or the one with the best sport reputation, or even the one with the most persistent recruiter. None of these strategies are ones I encourage my players to use. I want to make sure my athletes know that college is a *school*—a place for learning. Athletics may be a way to add enjoyment and challenge to the college experience and maybe even the means of paying the bill, but you should be very hesitant about making sports the guiding force behind your choice of schools.

SELECTION GUIDELINES

This chapter will take you step by step through a preliminary school selection process that ideally should be completed in the junior year. It will help you do two things: (1) choose schools that meet your academic and personal needs and (2) tie your athletic skills and goals to your top choices. But before you start the selection process, carefully consider these four guidelines:

Be Smart

Make sure you choose only schools that match your academic capabilities. It's certainly true that colleges and universities will waive admission requirements for recruited athletes, but once accepted the athlete is thrown into the academic pool with thousands of others who do meet the admission requirements. Athletes must compete with these better prepared students for good grades and they must meet the minimum academic standards set by their college and athletic association to remain eligible to play sports. That can be very difficult for athletes who are in over their heads. Be smart—remember, a college or university that requires a minimum combined SAT score of 1200 for admissions is not doing you a favor if they admit you despite your mere 850 combined score.

Be Realistic

Only the nation's best athletes are chosen for Division I teams. (See pages 113–116 for a complete discussion of athletic divisions.) This delegates the vast majority of American high school athletes to the less intense competition of Division II or III schools. Unfortunately for average athletes, it's the higher-level schools that offer the most scholarships. But that's because the competition is so intense for the best.

If you have been objectively evaluated as explained in Chapter One and seem to have NCAA Division I potential, I certainly encourage you to go for it. But, don't bank on it. Don't let yourself be left out of intercollegiate competition completely when a Division I placement doesn't come through. Always have back-up Division II or III schools or NAIA schools that also meet all the criteria you're looking for in an academic institution.

Be Choosey

Don't randomly scatter letters of inquiry all over the nation. This approach to choosing a college fosters the overwhelming and confusing feelings that make college selection so difficult. Use the process explained in this chapter to narrow the field of possibilities before contacting any schools. In this way you'll have a specific reason for wanting to know more about a school and will use the information you receive to clarify the selection process rather than obscure it.

On the other hand, don't sit around waiting for schools to contact you. No matter how talented, it's the prepared and aggressive athletes—the ones who know what they want and where they want to go—who are most likely to find the college that best matches their needs and abilities.

It's very tempting to accept the first offer of admission. This eliminates the time-consuming task of going through a detailed selection process—but don't. Scout around for other schools to compare things like cost, learning environment, teacher/student ratio and admission potential. Be choosey about your future.

Be Sure

Be sure you choose schools that will meet all your needs—not just your athletic ones. Make sure that the school will be right for you even if you get hurt and can't participate in your sport. Make sure you'll want to stay at the school even if you get cut from a team that needs to make room for some new hot-shot recruit. Many athletes burn out and quit their sport but still want to continue with their education. If this turn of events should happen during your college days, will you still want to stay at the school?

It's true that when things go wrong, athletes can transfer to other schools and sometimes this is the best recourse. But transferring is not always an easy option. Transfer students can lose one year's athletic eligibility; they often lose college credits; many lose time; and everyone loses money. So try to be sure that you would want to go to your chosen school even if you weren't an athlete.

FIVE FACTORS TO CONSIDER

When you begin your search for a college there are five factors that you should consider: academic suitability, cost, location, size of the student body and the athletic program. This section will explain why all these factors are important in making a comfortable match between a student and a school, and it will then help you select the schools you want to contact.

Academic Suitability

Academics should be the number-one consideration in choosing the schools you will eventually apply to. Although a few select colleges may be little more than training camps for the pros (see Goal 4, page 37), for all but a minuscule percentage of athletes college is still a place of higher learning where young men and women attain knowledge and skills that will enhance the quality of their lives after graduation. Too commonly I've seen high school athletes apply to schools solely because they've heard good things from fellow teammates who have gone there or from recruiters who have called, or even from moms and dads who went there themselves. However, because you have unique academic capabilities and needs, you should look very closely at the school's academic program before applying.

To begin the search for schools that match your individual academic strengths and weaknesses, you'll need an objective evaluation. Start with your school's guidance department. At the beginning of the junior year, make an appointment to meet with a guidance counselor. Explain your goal of finding a school where you can achieve academically and participate in intercollegiate sports. Get a written record of these three things: grade-point average (GPA), Preliminary Scholastic Aptitude Test (PSAT) or American College Test (ACT) scores and class rank (if an exact number is not available ask for a percentile estimate such as: "top 25 percent"). These numbers can be used to match a student's academic level to colleges where similar academic performance is the norm.*

If, for example, you have a GPA of 3.8 and/or a combined SAT score over 1350 or a composite ACT score of at least 32, you can certainly consider applying to the most selective schools such as one of the U.S. service academies, Princeton or Notre Dame.

If your GPA is between 2.5 and 3.5 and/or your combined SAT score is between 950 and 1350 or your composite ACT is between 19 and 32, you should consider moderately selective schools such as Michigan State, Boston University or Hofstra University.

---

* SAT and ACT scores listed in college guidebooks are most often *not* cut-off numbers. Usually they are "median" scores, which means that half the freshmen scored above that number and half scored below.

If your GPA is less than 2.0 and/or your combined SAT score is less than 900 or your composite ACT score is less than 19, you should restrict your choices to the least selective schools such as Indiana University–East, North Carolina–Wesleyan College or University of Texas–Dallas.

Because admission requirements are often bent to admit recruited athletes you can consider applying to schools that are above your academic standing—but be careful. If a men's basketball player with a combined 850 SAT score is admitted to Georgetown University, it doesn't take a rocket scientist to see that he'll have great difficulty meeting the NCAA academic eligibility requirements (never mind trying to learn something) in classes filled with students whose average SAT score is 1347. Even a four-year scholarship means little if the athlete can't make the grade in the classroom. Low grades equals no play so he loses out all around. If, however, this athlete takes his combined 850 and decides to seek acceptance at North Carolina State (which also has an excellent Division I basketball team) where the average combined SAT is 1050, he is making a more realistic choice.

On Worksheet 2 printed at the end of this chapter, you'll be instructed to list colleges that you might want to "reach" for despite a below-level academic record. When you select "reach" schools, use common sense and don't reach too high. Athletes who attend colleges that are completely out of their academic league continually prove the adage "The higher you go the harder you fall."

Finally, in considering the academic aspect of college selection, take time to consider possible fields of study. Many high school students don't know exactly what they want to choose as a major, but you should have an idea of an area of special interest. If, for example, you think you'd like to pursue a health-allied curriculum, you'll want to be sure that the colleges you choose to contact offer courses in this area. Or, if you think you might like to be either an engineer or a business entrepreneur, look for colleges that offer courses in both these areas. A full athletic scholarship to Arizona State is useless if you want to major in forestry.

Cost

The 1990s are difficult economic times that have brought with them soaring tuition costs and shrinking financial aid sources and awards. This factor may further limit the schools to which you apply.

At the time of this writing, expensive colleges are considered those whose cost* exceeds $12,000; moderately expensive ones are those costing between $5,000 and $12,000; and the least expensive ones cost under $5,000.

How much money can you afford to pay for your college education? Choose one of the above categories that you feel your family could pay in cash or with personal loans and record it on Worksheet 1, pages 38–39. If you hope to win an athletic scholarship to a particular school, put an R for *reach* next to that school in the cost column when you fill in Worksheet 2. Do the same if you expect to receive financial aid based on your family's income. Keep in mind as you fill out the chart that it's best to apply to no more than a total of four "reach" schools. Always include schools in your price range to fall back on if you don't get the scholarship or financial aid you'll need to attend the others.

Location

Every year young athletes tell me, "I'll go anywhere," but that answer is not a realistic one. No student can apply everywhere and when pressed to be more thoughtful, most will admit that they do have preferences. As part of the selection process, narrow your geographical preferences.

The distance consideration is especially important for athletes. If you choose a school that's too far to reach easily by car, your family will only rarely get to see you compete. You'll most likely come home only on major holidays and semester breaks, but even these visits can be cancelled due to athletic responsibilities. Also remember that distance from home also affects the total cost of college because air fares add up quickly.

---

* "Cost" refers to tuition, room and board; it does not include personal expenses such as clothing, entertainment or travel.

Climate likes and dislikes should also affect choice of location. You need to consider honestly if you could bear the long, cold winters of Minnesota, or the unceasing heat of Arizona or the unchanging climate of Florida. Do you want to be near the ocean? Do you like the change of seasons? Would you miss snow skiing? These things matter when it comes to picking a spot to spend the next four years.

A finer point of location analysis is whether the campus itself is in a rural, suburban or urban area. If you currently live in a country area, you might enjoy a visit to a noisy, hectic and large city, but could you live there happily day after day? Or, if you now live in an urban city area, could you comfortably adjust to a slower country pace with no real night life? To help you answer these questions, consider the following:

Consider urban schools if you agree with these statements:

- I love the fast pace of a big city.
- Country life is for hicks.
- I need to be near the cultural, entertainment and shopping opportunities offered in large cities.

Consider suburban schools if you agree with these statements:

- I like the idea of being able to find social activities both on and off campus.
- I'd like a country-like campus that's near a big city.
- I need to be near a shopping mall.

Consider rural schools if you agree with these statements:

- I like to hike, camp, fish or cycle in my free time.
- I like it when everybody knows everybody else.
- I need wide open spaces and quiet.

These distinctions are stated in most college guidebooks and college-selection computer programs. They're quite accurate with one exception: If you don't want to go to a big city school, be lenient with those labeled "urban." Record them as reach schools and, if they remain on your final selection chart, visit the campus before you rule them out completely. There are many beautiful, ivy-covered campuses that sit smack in the middle of large urban areas. Columbia University, for example, is in the middle of New York City and is labeled "urban" in guidebooks. But the campus itself sits quietly behind guarded iron gates. I recently met a young woman who had an opportunity to compete on the swim team at this very selective school but was looking elsewhere because she didn't like what she'd heard about New York. Finally she reluctantly agreed to take a look and came home hooked. The campus itself is quaint; the buildings are surrounded by winding tree-lined paths, and the students this young lady met were easy-going and friendly. Sometimes "urban" does mean tall buildings on busy streets, but sometimes it doesn't.

One last location consideration is an economic one. Some areas of the country are more expensive to live in than others—college costs generally mimic these cost-of-living trends. Because it's more expensive to live in the northeastern United States than in the southeastern areas, for example, students who are looking to go to an out-of-state college or university should look south to save money. For instance, according to *Barron's Profiles of American Colleges* (18th ed. Barron's Educational Series, Inc., 1991), the University of Rhode Island, which is a large, public university, cost out-of-state students $10,805 for tuition, room and board in 1991. A similar large, public university, the University of North Carolina–Charlotte, cost in that same year $7,348. Both schools offer NCAA Division I intercollegiate male and female athletic programs and both offer comparable educations—the degree from either school will offer the same postgraduate opportunities. Yet over four years, the degree from Rhode Island will cost $13,828 more than the one from North Carolina. It's certainly worthwhile to consider cost when narrowing down location.

Size

College size is determined by the number of undergraduate students in attendance. As a general rule, size classifications follow these guidelines:

small = less than 3,000 students
medium = between 3,000 and 12,000 students
large = more than 12,000 students

Although you might at first say, "I don't care about size," the size of the institution can have a dramatic effect on the learning environment. Small colleges tend to give students more personalized attention, more access to library, computer and laboratory resources, and less registration and housing hassles. But on the other hand, students have little privacy, a limited range of social activities and less exposure to state-of-the-art technological resources.

At large universities students experience a more diverse student body and roster of social activities and often have access to highly specialized and up-to-date laboratory, computer and library resources. However, in large universities classes run on the crowded side (lecture classes may hold 300 to 1,000 students), personal attention is scarce and freshman and sophomore students are often instructed by graduate student assistants and fellows. Also keep in mind that to pay for the latest in equipment, research facilities and graduate programs, tuition at public universities is generally 25 percent more than at public colleges, and about 50 percent more at private universities than at private colleges.

The medium-size college or university offers a sampling of the good and bad of both the larger and smaller schools. These schools offer a wide diversity of students but not so many that you never see the same face twice. Students are not closely supervised but professors are reasonably accessible. The cost, too, usually falls between the two extremes.

Athletic Program

After you have considered your academic abilities and preferences in college costs, location and size, you'll have a clearer picture of where you'll be able to excel as a student and live in personal comfort regardless of athletic standing. Once that's accomplished it's time to add athletic considerations to the school selection equation. On Worksheet 1, pages 38–39, fill in the sport you'd like to play and the division level the coaches have suggested is most appropriate.

The National Collegiate Athletic Association (NCAA) divides the sports programs in its over 400 member schools into three divisions. A most important difference among the divisions concerns the awarding of athletic scholarships. Division I sports are allowed to offer more scholarships than Division II sports which most often offer only partial scholarships or none at all. Division III sports are not allowed to offer any scholarships based on athletic ability. Because of these scholarship rules, the Division I programs claim the very best high school athletes with their financial enticements. Naturally these best players make up the best and most competitive teams.

Within a given NCAA school different sports may compete on different divisional levels. Before assuming that because the school plays Division I football they also play Division I golf, be sure to check with the individual coaches. If football is your sport, you should also know that the top-level NCAA football teams are divided into Division I-A and Division I-AA, with I-A encompassing the most competitive programs that offer media exposure and often produce future professional players.

Record the division level the coach has recommended for you on Worksheets 1 and 2. If, however, the coach has recommended Division II, but you're intent on trying for a Division I school, put the school down on Worksheet 2 as a reach school. But remember, the selection process allows you a total of only four reaches.

There are about 425 four-year colleges—mostly small and medium sized—that belong *not* to the NCAA, but to the National Association of Intercollegiate Athletics (NAIA). (Some schools belong to both.) This is a completely autonomous association that governs the athletic programs for males and females in its member schools, which are organized into 32 geographic districts throughout the United States. The schools are not divided into competitive divisions that easily compare to the NCAA divisions; rather, association representatives feel that the competitive level of their programs can be assessed by noting the size of the institution—the larger the school the more competitive the sport. Although not a scientific fact, a general rule of thumb says that NAIA Division I schools are comparable to NCAA Division II schools. All NAIA schools are allowed to offer athletic scholarships, but not all choose to do so. If you're interested in a school that you find belongs to the NAIA, contact the athletic director for complete information about its competitive level and scholarship opportunities.

ATHLETIC GOALS

To assure a good match between a college and your athletic interests, ask yourself why you want to compete in intercollegiate athletics. Your goals can help narrow down the list of schools you should contact. There are four common athletic goals you might find yourself pursuing:

Goal #1: To Enhance College Admission Opportunities

Many high school athletes use their physical skills to open college doors that would otherwise be closed to them. This includes students like Jeff whose poor academic record made it very difficult for him to meet the admission standards at even local, state colleges. Jeff, however, was able to use his soccer skills to enter through the back door of the athletic department at a nearby Division III school. He's quite aware that without soccer he never would have been accepted.

This goal is also used by exceptionally bright students who want to improve their chances of being admitted to highly selective schools. Ivy League hopeful, Dorrie, took her track record to the coaches of the finest schools and gained admission to the university of her choice. Perhaps her academic record alone would have granted her admission, but Dorrie felt track gave her the boost she needed to be considered over the thousands of other applicants.

If your academic record is so very poor that even sports can't help you gain admission to a four-year college, you should consider an alternate route through a two-year college. See Chapter Ten for more information about junior and community colleges.

Goal #2: To Gain an Athletic Scholarship

Competing for an athletic scholarship is like competing in a national championship. You're up against the best and no matter how good you think you are the fact is you might lose. The outcome has a lot to do with how well trained and prepared you are and how aggressively you pursue the goal. Some highly recruited, blue-chip athletes get so many scholarship offers it's hard for them to choose the best one. But for the rest of the nation's athletes, scholarship money has to be fought for. Chapters One, Two and Four explain how to get into the fight, but you still need to choose carefully the schools that you'll approach for money. Pursuing a scholarship at a school that's across the country and doesn't offer the academic program you're interested in, for example, will be a waste of time and effort if travel and phone expenses eat up a year's worth of tuition money and you're left with a degree in a field you couldn't care less about.

The scholarship goal will also narrow down the schools you'll choose to contact. Ivy League and NCAA Division III schools don't give athletic scholarships. But, some NAIA Division III schools do give scholarships and many NCAA and Ivy League schools put together rather creative financial aid packages for athletes. So if you're looking for scholarship money, don't rule out Division IIIs and Ivys completely. Put them down on your worksheet as reach schools. If money is your goal, you have a lot of digging and fighting to do—but the money is out there. So if you have the skill, use the information in Chapter Eight to go after it.

Goal #3: To Compete

Some high school athletes just want to keep competing. They don't really care where; they just love to practice their sport and don't want to give it up when they go to college. If this sounds like you, you can play the recruiting game at any school that matches your academic profile. You should, however, shy away from highly compet-itive schools where you'll have to fight continually for a starting position and where many talented athletes sit on the bench.

If you aren't signed by any recruiters at the schools of your choice, you should certainly look into the alternative routes to athletic play explained in Chapter Ten, which include joining as a walk-on or playing on club or intramural teams.

Goal #4: To Make It to the Pros

Goal #4 can be called the exception to all rules. If you want to play intercollegiate athletics solely as a launching pad to the pros, you may need to choose colleges and universities that have the reputations as pro training camps, not the ones that necessarily meet your personal and academic needs. You'll want to contact schools where TV exposure is plentiful, where sports reporters camp out, and where competition is keen and pro-like. It is here where academics are not always number one, and the number of athletes who actually graduate is often minimal. These include schools such as football's Michigan State, baseball's Arizona State, and basketball's University of Nevada–Las Vegas.

If you're a good candidate for these schools, you won't have to ask to be invited. The athletes who go to these schools are heavily recruited because they are the very best. But even if you're a blue-chip athlete, before you're tempted to take this road consider the possible outcome: no pro career and no college diploma. Statistics compiled by the Center for Sports and Society at North-eastern University make it clear that this goal is a gamble. They report that the National Basketball Association, for example, has only 48 openings each year and 4,400 top-level college seniors to choose from. Moreover, even those who make the NBA have a less than 40 percent chance of remaining on the team for three years. Obviously, although college sports can pave the way to stardom, even athletes headed for the pros should select schools that offer them a secure future outside the sports arena. A college degree works for a lifetime; an athlete works for a very short time.

WORKSHEET #1

I. On another piece of paper, list all the colleges you would consider attending.

II. ACADEMIC STATISTICS
Grade Point Average: _____
SAT scores: Verbal _____ Math _____
ACT scores:
Class Rank: _____
Possible major: _____

III. IDEAL COLLEGE

1. COST

I am willing to pay (tuition, room and board):
a) more than $12,000
b) between $5,000 and $12,000
c) less than $5,000

2. LOCATION

I want to attend a school in:
a) the Northeast   e) the Southwest
b) the Southeast   f) Hawaii
c) the Midwest   g) Alaska
d) the Northwest   h) Puerto Rico

Although your reasons for wanting to participate in a collegiate sport may affect your choice of schools, you should still use a rational approach when choosing ones to contact. Remember:

- Always include back-up schools on your list of colleges to contact. Coaches and recruiters do lie; they may promise you a place on the team and a scholarship but then drop you. Coaches also know that young athletes lie too; they promise to come to their school and then change their mind. So to protect themselves from being left with an open slot they may present

I'd prefer a school in:
 a) a rural area
 b) a suburban area
 c) an urban area

IV. SIZE

I'd feel most comfortable in a:
 a) small college (less than 3,000 students)
 b) medium-size school (between 3,000 and 12,000 students)
 c) large university (more than 12,000 students)

V. ATHLETICS

I want to compete in intercollegiate (insert name of sport)

_____

I want to apply to Division _____ schools.
I would play for a school belonging to the NAIA.
 yes ____ no ____
I am hoping athletics will boost my chances of getting admitted to the college or university of my choice.
 yes ____ no ____
I want an athletic scholarship.
 yes ____ no ____
I just want to compete in my sport.
 yes ____ no ____
I want to move on to the pros.
 Yes ____ no ____

the admissions committee with a number of possible recruits knowing they'll only get one. If you're not that one, you're out. Make sure you have some place else to go.

- Don't let recruiters distract you from your personal and academic needs. If a school representative contacts you, put the school on your worksheet and see if it matches your criteria. If it doesn't, cross the school off the list.

- Play offense. *You* find the schools. *You* contact these schools. Then *you* sell your talents in the places you want to be.

MATCHING SCHOOLS AND ATHLETES

Once you've filled in all the blanks on Worksheet 1, move those pieces of information to the appropriate spaces on Worksheet 2. Then list down the left margin of Worksheet 2 all the schools that you might like to attend. List ones you might consider by reputation, family, friend or alumni recommendations, or those suggested by guidance counselors. Now you can match the characteristics of these schools to the ones you have listed across the top.

You can find the information to fill in the blanks for each school in college guidebooks. Of the many on the market, I use two that are most informative for the student-athlete. *Peterson's Four-Year Colleges* gives an easy-to-use comparative chart that lists vital statistics such as SAT/ACT information and enrollment numbers; it also has a directory of college majors. Then in informative state-by-state summaries, the book details important factors such as entrance level of difficulty, cost and percentage of admitted students who scored over a given SAT score. This guide also lists all intercollegiate sports offered at each school, their association and division, and the availability of athletic scholarships.

Another guidebook, *GIS Guide to Four-Year Colleges*, offers a state-by-state comparative chart listing setting, size, campus type, cost and selectivity index; it too has a curriculum majors index and it lists the intercollegiate sports and divisions played at each institution. This book is the printed companion of the computerized Guidance Information System available in many high school guidance departments. If this service or any other college selection computer program is available to you, give it a try! You can type in your personal criteria and the program will print out all the schools that match. Certainly a time-saving piece of technology.

Either way, guidebook or computer, there are resources available that will help you fill in Worksheet 2. Because it's quite expensive to buy these books and software programs, check first at your local libraries and your high school's guidance department; there the reference material is probably yours for the asking. (Make sure it is current. The statistics can change drastically from year to year.)

When you have examined all the schools that were on your original list against the criteria you've listed on the top of Worksheet 2, it's time to look actively for more schools. Now that you have a good idea of the kind of school you're looking for, use the guidebooks, computer programs, college fairs and local alumni representatives to add to your list. When you're satisfied that you've evaluated each carefully and eliminated all that don't fit the picture, you can then make a new list of the ones you'll contact. The following chapters will guide you through the recruiting and application process until, in Chapter Nine, you'll be ready to make the final choice.

Larry Bird was not the first nor the last young athlete to choose the wrong college; there seems to be a great deal of mismatching still going on among athletes and colleges. A newly released study by the NCAA has found that of 3,288 athletes in 85 Division I schools who entered college in 1984 and 1985 only 45.7 percent graduated. (In addition, only 26.6 percent of the black athletes in this group received diplomas.) There's no way to assign a simple or single reason to these dismal numbers, but they do serve as a warning to prospective college athletes. Choosing the right school means choosing a school that meets all your needs—not just your athletic ones.

WORKSHEET #2

DIRECTIONS: Use a college guidebook or computer program to match each college you list down the left margin of this worksheet with your criteria listed across the top line. Put an "R" for "reach" under cost each time you would attend only if given a scholarship or financial aid. Do the same under academics when you could attend the school only if admission requirements are waived for your athletic skills. Insert "NA" if you have no answer because the category is inconsequential to you. Look over Roy Hopkins' sample entry before you begin.

	Academics	Major	Cost	Location	Campus Type	Sport/Div.	Scholarship	Contact
Roy	850 SAT	Communications	<$12,000	East Coast	suburban/rural	Baseball II	yes	
Boston University	1145 X	✓	$21,125 X	✓	urban X	Div.I X	✓	no
Slippery Rock U.	934 ✓	✓	$6,680 ✓	✓	✓	✓	✓	yes!

✓ = a match   x = no match

CONTACTING COLLEGE COACHES

Tom Seaver was not one of the stars on his high school baseball team and was not recruited to play college ball. *The Sports Factory* (Joseph Durso, Quadrangle Pub., 1975) reports that he went to a junior college in Fresno, California, but coaches from the four-year colleges still ignored him. Finally, tired of waiting to be discovered, Seaver called the coach at the University of Southern California and asked for an athletic scholarship. Because Seaver was a virtual unknown, the coach asked him to try out in their scouting league in Fairbanks, Alaska. There he gave an impressive performance and got his U.S.C. scholarship. Because Tom Seaver aggressively went after what he wanted, he became one of the best pitchers in professional baseball.

Then and now, college coaches can't keep track of all the talented high school athletes in this country. So take a lesson from Tom Seaver and contact the coaches at the colleges where you'd like to participate in a sport.

YOUR RESUME

Once you've put together a list of 50 to 100 schools that match your academic and athletic needs, let the coaches at these schools know you're interested by sending out a well prepared and organized five-part resume that includes (1) personal and academic information, (2) an athletic profile, (3) news clippings, (4) recommendations, and (5) a cover letter.

Part I: Personal and Academic Information

When you contact a college coach, always put academics first. If the academic record is good, it shows off your priorities and capabilities. If the record is poor, it puts that information right up front where the coach can weigh it against the strengths of the athletic record. There's no place to hide academic weaknesses in the college admissions process, so don't try—these facts have to be considered in the evaluation and placement of all student-athletes.

The resume you're putting together is not a college application (that will come later), so you don't yet need to send along a lengthy or official transcript. Give the coaches the basic information they need by neatly listing personal information on the top of the first page of your resume. Include: name, address, phone number, height, weight, age and birthdate. Then list academic information such as grade-point average, class rank, SAT or ACT scores and graduation date. Include any advanced placement classes or academic honors, and note future academic interests. On the bottom of this first page give an overview of your school; this helps coaches get a general picture of where students compete both academically and athletically. Note the school type (public, private, co-ed), size (number of students) and location.

Roy, the student whose college-choice list was used as an example in Chapter Three, drew up this academic information sheet:

PERSONAL

Roy Hopkins
49 Shepard Lane
Hawthorne, New Jersey
(201) 423-0000

Hawthorne High School
Parmelee Ave.
Hawthorne, NJ 07506
(201) 423-0000

height: 6'4"
weight: 205 lbs.
age: 16 (7/12/00)

ACADEMICS

GPA: 3.766
Class Rank: 9 out of 148
SAT Scores: Math: 560   Verbal: 320
Graduation date: June 1993

Honors:

National Honor Society
Honors Courses: English and history
Advanced Placement Courses: Math
Future academic interest: Business

Part II: Athletic Profile

The athletic profile contains information that helps coaches evaluate an athlete's intercollegiate potential. To introduce your athletic accomplishments, put your school's conference or league on the top of page two and note that you've enclosed a schedule of upcoming competitions. This page of the resume should focus on the one sport you want to play in college. If ice hockey is your goal, don't confuse the issue by listing awards in soccer. If you feel the "other" sport is a complementary one or is an indication of further athletic skill, simply list it at the bottom.

On this athletic profile page be sure to list all leagues and competitions you participate in. Also include all relevant statistics, awards and honors.

Roy's athletic profile looked like this:

ROY HOPKINS
Athletic Profile

Sport: Baseball
Conference: Bergen-Passaic Scholastic League (BPSL)
Position: Pitcher   Speed: Lower to mid 80s
Throws: Right   Control: Very good
Arm: Excellent   Pitches: F.B., curve, fork, sinker
A varsity schedule is enclosed and a videotape is available.
Hawthorne High School Varsity Team
Starter: Sophomore year
Stats:

W	L	ERA	IP	Comp. G.	Shut O.	BB	H	K	2B	3B	HR	RS	ER
6	1	0.98	43	6	3	21	18	56	7	1	0	15	6

Honors: 1st Team All League (sophomore year)
American Legion Summer League
Starter: Freshman and sophomore years
Stats: (Sophomore year)

W	L	ERA	IP	Comp. G.	Shut O.	BB	H	K	2B	3B	HR	RS	ER
5	5	1.20	55	8	4	30	21	80	7	2	0	18	9

Honors: All-Star Team (freshman and sophomore years)
Rochland County Fall League
Starter: Sophomore year
Stats:

W	L	ERA	IP	Comp. G.	Shut O.	BB	H	K	2B	3B	HR	RS	ER
5	0	0.58	32	4	0	18	16	52	4	2	1	10	6

Other Sports: Varsity basketball sophomore and junior years

Part III: News Clippings

Sometimes news clippings can sway a coach's decision to actively recruit an athlete; other times they can bore a coach to the point of total disinterest. If you have kept news clippings of your athletic adventures through the years, now is the time to gather them together and pick out a few special ones. As you begin to weed the good from the ordinary keep these guidelines in mind:

- Include clippings of one sport only.
- Include clippings of secondary level events only.
- Include articles that focus on you, not the team or the game.
- Include clippings about special awards or recognition.
- Do not include box scores, team reports or routine coverage.

Make clear copies of your chosen few (no more than five). Then use a highlight pen to draw attention to your name on every copy. (Don't highlight the original newsprint; the highlighter will blacken the line on the copy and make it very difficult to read.)

Take all your leftover articles and put them together in a scrapbook. If a recruiter should come to your home or school, you can show them at that time. But in the resume that you send unsolicited to college coaches, be choosey and limit the number.

Part IV: Athletic Recommendations

Recommendations are not an absolutely necessary part of the resume package. They are helpful only if they are written by an objective third party with appropriate credentials. A coach from a rival team, for example, may be willing to offer unbiased praise. A coach from a clinic or camp can give a technical evaluation. And an umpire, referee or tournament judge who has watched you play or perform can also offer valuable insight into your athletic abilities. But a subjective recommendation from a family friend or a school administrator is not necessary or even helpful.

The way you ask for a letter of recommendation can affect the quality of what you get. Choose someone you feel admires your talent. Then contact that person and explain exactly what the letter is for. Because the statistics on the athletic profile speak for themselves, ask for recommendations that not only attest to athletic skill but also specifically mention qualities like perserverence, determination and leadership abilities. This is perhaps the only opportunity college coaches have to learn something about your attitude and work ethic. These two factors are very important in the collegiate athletic arena where there's little time or patience to waste on hotheads or primadonnas.

Roy Hopkins asked his fall league coach for a letter of recommendation. Because this person has the credentials to judge athletic ability and because the letter (which is printed on the following page) mentions Roy's attitude, he chose to include it in his resume.

Part V: Cover Letter

After you have put together your academic information sheet, athletic profile, news clippings and recommendations, it's time to write a cover letter for this packet. This letter is written directly to the college coach; it introduces the athlete and explains that you are interested in participating in an intercollegiate athletic program. Make sure the letter notes any camps or clinics you will be attending off-season and remind the coach that a schedule is enclosed (even if it's a tentative one, say so and enclose it).

The letter can be written by you or your coach. I have spoken with college coaches who say they prefer to hear directly from the athletes and others who say they'd rather initially correspond with the coach. At this early stage it doesn't really matter who writes the letter. But how it looks and reads does matter.

Try to keep the cover letter from looking like a form letter. Coaches are often put off by sloppily copied forms that they know are being sent out all over the nation. If you have the time, personalize each letter by mentioning the name of the college and a few reasons why that school fits your needs and goals. In a random survey of college coaches that I took while writing this book, all responding coaches said they always pay attention to letters that show the athletes have considered the college's academic program and already know that it fits their educational goals. Although it's nice to personalize the letter by using a

SAMPLE LETTER OF RECOMMENDATION

Dear Sir,

I am writing this letter of recommendation on behalf of Roy Hopkins. As a brief introduction, I am the president of the New Jersey Amateur Conference Senior Division (15-year-olds to unlimited age). I am a manager in the Suburban Stan Musial Baseball League (unlimited age) as well as a coach in the Rockland County Fall Baseball League. Based on these activities I believe I have reliable information on the most talented high school and college baseball players in the northern New Jersey area.

I first had the pleasure of coaching Roy through my involvement with the fall baseball league. Up to that time I knew Roy only through his fine performance on his high school team and his summer Legion team. In coaching Roy I feel confident in saying he is one of the more promising high school ball players in northern New Jersey. He is an extremely gifted pitcher with command of a variety of pitches. He has been very effective in fall league play and has a win/loss record of 4–1 with a 0.58 ERA.

In addition to his fine athletic ability, Roy is very easy to coach. He listens carefully to suggestions and is open minded. He also mixes well with the other players on his team and is a positive influence on the bench.

In sum, I would highly recommend Roy to your baseball program and college. If you would like to discuss Roy further please contact me at home (201) 423-0000, or at work (201) 855-0000.

Sincerely,

Angelo J. Cifaldi

coach's name, don't use the names given in college guide books or even in the *Directory of College Athletics*, coaches move frequently from one school to another before the books even make it to print. Unless you are absolutely sure of the head coach's name, address your letter: "Dear Coach." Make sure the cover letter is neatly typed and proofread for spelling, grammar and typo errors. If possible, use a word processor and a letter-quality printer.

The letter I wrote for Roy is printed below. It certainly is not the only kind of letter that can go out with your resume, but use it as a guideline. If the coach is writing your letter, you might make a copy

SAMPLE COVER LETTER

Dear Coach,

I'm sending you an academic and athletic profile of a baseball player, Roy Hopkins. Although Roy is only a junior in high school, I have no doubt that he has the potential to be an outstanding pitcher on the Division I level.

Roy started for me as a varsity pitcher in his sophomore year and was extremely successful, ending the season with a 6-1 record and an ERA of 0.98. He possesses all the attributes necessary to be an outstanding player. He is smart and coachable and has developed an impressive work ethic on and off the field. I feel Roy is one of the best players in the area and would be an asset to any college or university baseball program.

I've enclosed a tentative schedule for our upcoming season. If you need more information please call me at the high school or at home.

Sincerely,

Jack DiSalvo
Head Baseball Coach
Hawthorne High School
Hawthorne, NJ 07506
(201) 423-0000
(201) 554-0000 (Home)

of this sample letter, put it together with your academic and athletic profiles and give it to the coach. These pieces of information will help the coach create an initial impression that is accurate and up to date, and serves the same purpose as a strong handshake.

TIMING

Timing is key in playing a successful recruiting game. Send your resume off too early and coaches, still trying to recruit athletes for the upcoming season, may set it aside for later review and then forget or lose it. Send it too late and coaches are likely to have already filled their team vacancies and/or distributed their alloted scholarship money. Send it just when they're getting ready to go looking for talent and you'll fall right into their recruiting schedule.

CONTACT CALENDAR Junior Year		
Spring Sports* Dec. Jan. Feb.	Fall Sports March April May	Winter Sports June July Aug. Sept.
baseball crew golf lacrosse softball tennis track and field	cross country field hockey football soccer volleyball water polo	basketball fencing gymnastics ice hockey squash swimming track and field wrestling

* The contact period for spring sports is early in the junior year because if a spring athlete waits until the end of the junior year to contact college coaches, the coaches and recruiters may not have an opportunity to watch the athlete before the application and admissions deadlines the following year. That's why Roy Hopkins' athletic resume included only his sophomore-year stats; his resume was sent out before he played his junior-year season.

That "just-right" time depends on the season of your sport (see the chart on page 51) but there are a few general rules that remain constant. Plan to make your contacts in your junior year. If you're contacting NCAA schools be sure to keep in mind their contact and evaluation periods explained in Chapter Five. In some sports there are restrictions on when, how and how often coaches and recruiters can contact or evaluate a young athlete. A college representative from an NCAA Division I or II sport can contact a prospective student/athlete by mail, for example, no sooner than September 1 of the junior year, and no one can meet in person with an athlete, on or off campus, until on or after July 1 at the end of the athlete's junior year. So although there is no restriction on when an athlete can send a resume to a coach, don't expect a visit or a phone call as soon as you send your packets out. During noncontact periods, coaches sometimes choose to correspond with the athlete's coach or they may decide simply to keep an eye on the athlete and make contact after the junior year.

Of course, if at any time you receive a letter of interest from a college coach, use a guidebook to put the school's vital statistics on your Worksheet from Chapter Three and if there's a match, send out your resume immediately.

These contact periods are not official or inflexible. They are only guidelines that give you an idea of schedules that enhance your chances of being chosen to play on a collegiate team. There are certainly exceptions. Sophomore athletes, for example, who show exceptional talent, are seemingly destined for top-level intercollegiate competition and know where they want to go to college, should by all means make their contacts early. They should also follow up with reminder letters in their junior year to any schools they haven't heard from. Or, if on the other hand you don't decide to pursue college athletics until after these contact periods are long past, don't give up—hurry up. To maximize your time limitations, use the telephone. Call the head coaches at the schools you've chosen, explain that you would like to participate in their athletic program and ask if the coach would look over a personal resume. Send them by overnight mail if possible. Although a late contact does reduce an athlete's chances of making the team and of receiving scholarship money, it doesn't rule it out entirely.

You can expect to hear back from at least 50 percent of the coaches you contact. Be sure to reply back to *all* those who do contact you. If the response is bad news—"We can't use you"—send a note thanking the coach for taking time to consider the resume. Some coaches may not be looking for an athlete that matches your position, size, record or whatever; others may rely solely on their recruiters to find new athletes. But needs have a way of changing unexpectedly and if a coach finds later in the admissions process that he or she is still an athlete short, a polite response to initial rejection may pay off.

If, after one month, you don't hear anything from schools that you're especially interested in, have your coach call the college coach. Ask him or her to explain that you have not received any response to the resume, but because the school is very high on your list you'd like to send along a videotape. The answer may be "no" but at least you'll know for sure.

If the response is good news—"We'd like to know more about you"—most coaches will request to see a videotape of your athletic performance.

VIDEOTAPES

Athletic videotapes help college coaches decide which athletes they'll actively recruit and evaluate in person. Although you can hire a professional to make these tapes (you can find this service by inquiring at photography stores listed in the yellow pages of the phone book), if you or your school's audio-visual department have a video camera, you can save quite a bit of money by doing it yourself.

The contents of a videotape depends on the sport you compete in. If you participate in a sport that involves one-on-one matches like tennis, squash, wrestling or fencing, or can be judged by individual records such as in swimming, track events, gymnastics, golf or skiing, you can send college coaches a tape of an athletic performance at a match or meet. Obviously it's best to film several competitions and choose the best one, but also remember that college coaches want to see the highest level of competition you can handle. So if, for example, you have one tape on which you win an easy 6-0, 6-0 tennis match, and another on which you triumphant in a 6-4, 4-6, 6-2 match—assuming skill and style are displayed equally—the more competitive one is the better choice.

If you play a team sport, it's usually best not to send a college coach a tape of an entire game. It's very boring to watch a team player stand around waiting for action. If you have no other choice but to send a complete game tape, at the very least help the college coach catch the highlights. Write a letter that sets the stage for watching the game. Include the name of the other team, their record for the year and any interesting anecdotes about the game. Tell the coach the color uniform and number you're wearing and most importantly where on the tape you are most actively involved. To find the sections that make the best viewing, put the tape in a VCR, set the counter on zero and as you watch the tape, jot down the numbers where the coach can see the best stuff. Fast forwarding to the right spots makes a coach's job much easier and more effective.

Ideally, an athletic tape should include a little bit of everything. It should include highlights from games and competitions as well as footage of drills and practice. To get the best tape, record three or four entire athletic events. Then arrange with the high school coach to tape a practice that focuses on you. Your coach may even be able to arrange a practice session just for you and a few key players. If you're filming softball practice, for example, have a good pitcher throw you a hundred or so balls to hit. Get some fielding footage that shows you grabbing line drives and scooping up grounders and then throwing them over to first. Or, if you're filming football, run some plays, run the ball down field, and even hit the dummies and do agilities. These clips will give a coach some insight into your skill and drive.

When you're satisfied that you've gotten a good representation of your skills, it's time to put the best onto one tape. To do this, set your VCR counter at zero and watch each tape. Note the beginning and end number of each section you want to keep for the final tape. If you have two VCRs of your own you can create the final product yourself, but because home editing usually looks amateurish, this is one time it pays to have professionals do the job. Bring your tapes and numbers to a photography store that edits and splices videotape and let them make you a polished product.

Once you have the final tape, you'll need to make copies to send to all the coaches who have requested one. If you or the school have two VCRs you can save money by using them to make these copies. If you have to have them commercially copied, it will be expensive (see estimated prices below) so you might want to send out only a few at a time with a prepaid return mailer and a request that the tape be returned to you as soon as possible. Be sure to keep the original so you can make more copies; many of your tapes won't be returned.

The cost of making an athletic videotape varies not only by geographical location but even from store to store. So shop around by calling photography stores and asking for price information. A survey of stores in my northern New Jersey area came up with these average prices: $30 per day for video camera rental (with $1,000 deposit on a charge card number that is never recorded unless the camera isn't returned), $60 for editing several tapes down to one tape with titles and music, and $20 for one copy.

Athletic videotapes can be somewhat time consuming and costly to make, but don't underestimate their value. As the numbers of talented athletes increases and recruiting budgets decrease, these tapes are more and more frequently used by college coaches as their primary initial evaluation tool. Along with an organized resume, the videotape is to the sports recruiting arena what an impressive resume and experience portfolio are in the world of career placement. They speak for you before you're given an opportunity to speak for yourself. It's worth your time and effort to make sure that your resume and tape speak highly of your skills, potential and desire.

ATHLETIC PLACEMENT SERVICES

Just as there are employment services that help people find a job, there are athletic placement services that help high school athletes find a spot on a college team. Following the same steps explained in this chapter, most placement officers help athletes compile a resume that includes academic information, an athletic profile and coaches' evaluations. Then, under their own cover letter, they send out these information packets to selected colleges and follow up positive responses with videotapes supplied by the athlete. Whether you contact college coaches yourself or have a placement service do it, the process is the same.

A placement service can be most beneficial to athletes who are unsure of their athletic competitive level and/or are having trouble matching athletic and academic needs. A reputable service like New Jersey's College Athletic Placement Service (CAPS) counsels young athletes and evaluates their capabilities to help them make a satisfactory match. CAPS does not charge a fee for the initial hour-long interview in which director Bill Serra meets with the athlete and his or her parents to gather information about the athlete's academic standing and athletic successes and goals. Using the academic transcript, coaches' evaluations, sport statistics and a videotape of an athletic performance, Serra decides if the athlete has college potential. Only then, if the athlete shows promise, will Serra charge a fee and agree to try to place the athlete. CAPS is an example of a respectable and successful agency, but if you're thinking about using a placement service, beware: not all agencies are as thorough or as personal.

Because many placement services haphazardly send out hundreds of inquiries without any consideration of an athlete's goals, competitive level and academic abilities, many coaches have become leery about responding to commercially prepared resumes. Sharon Goldbrenner, head coach of Trenton State's national championship field hockey and lacrosse teams, echos the feelings of many coaches when she says, "I'm finding commercial placement inquiries to be wasteful. To respond back to these kids all over the country takes a lot of time and it usually happens that most of the kids aren't really interested in my school. I'd much prefer a personal contact from the athlete or the parents. If I had a son or daughter I would not use a placement service."

Random solicitation annoys the coaches and rarely reaps positive results. Most often athletes get no more for their money from a placement service than they can get for free from their guidance department or local library. Some agencies, for example, claim to use a computerized system to match athletes and colleges according to level of ability, academic record, geographical location and desired major. What you get back is the same information you can get from the guidance computer programs and the college guidebooks recommended in Chapter Three. If you're looking for more, make sure you ask exactly what services are offered before you put down your money.

If you take the time to follow the recruiting process explained in each chapter of this book, there is nothing an agency can do that you can't do yourself. But if you do choose to try your luck with a placement service, first consider these two indications that you aren't getting your money's worth: First, something is wrong if the service doesn't offer you a personal interview. If the deal is "Fill out this form and send us your money," you can be sure that attention to your needs and goals is not a priority at this agency. Second, it's bogus for any agency to guarantee satisfactory placement. True, a placement service can probably find some school somewhere with some kind of athletic program for you, but that's not the goal. Higher education at a college well suited to your ability and needs is the goal; athletics can be the means to get there and enjoy the experience. Don't let any placement representative mix up these priorities.

Contacting college coaches is a big job, but once it's done you're on your way to finding a spot on a college team. Next, you need to be prepared for your entrance into the recruiting process by learning the recruiting rules and regulations that govern intercollegiate athletic programs. You'll find this information in the next chapter.

UNDERSTANDING ATHLETIC RULES AND REGULATIONS

On November 10, 1990 during the official paid visit to the university's campus by a prospective student-athlete, the men's head basketball coach allowed the young man and his father to visit a skybox at the Hubert H. Humphrey Metrodome (Minneapolis, Minnesota) for a portion of the football game between the University of Minnesota and Michigan State University. The prospect and his father also were introduced to a representative of the university's athletics interests during the football game.

The above portion of a news release issued by the National Collegiate Athletic Association in March 1991 sounds at first like a description of a cordial campus visit. Unfortunately, it is exerpted from the infractions report issued against the University of Minnesota for recruiting violations. Whether or not the boy and his dad knew it at the time, the coach was entertaining them in ways that violated NCAA rules and regulations and so jeopardized the athlete's eligibility to play at the university and risked the competitive future of the college team. The coach, the athlete and the basketball team were all eventually penalized.

The moment you are contacted by a college coach you become an official player in the recruiting game. As the story above illustrates—if you're going to play the game, you'd better know the rules. So while you're waiting to hear from the coaches you contacted through the process outlined in the last chapter, take some time to study the rules and regulations that govern intercollegiate recruiting and eligibility.

THE PURPOSE OF REGULATIONS

Each athletic association and conference has established rules to protect young recruits. The rules regarding academic eligibility attempt to guarantee that the college experience is an academic as well as an athletic one. The recruiting regulations protect young students from the exploitive and unethical practices that coaches and recruiters are sometimes tempted to use to pursuade talented athletes to choose their school over all others. And the policies regarding amateur status ensure that the distinction between collegiate and professional athletes remains clear cut.

INFRACTIONS AND PENALTIES

The most pressing reason to obey the rules of athletic associations is the fact that it's unethical and dishonest to cheat the athletic system. But because it's impossible to guarantee the scruples of all coaches and athletes, each association has established regulations and enforcement procedures that try to regulate the activities of all athletic representatives.

Once you're in the recruiting game, ignorance of the rules is no excuse for breaking them. Although college coaches who break recruiting regulations jeopardize their own jobs, if they break them while trying to attract you to their school, you may also pay a price.

Consider the 1989 recruiting fiasco at the University of Kentucky. A basketball coach at the university sent a $1,000 "gift" by overnight mail to a high school athlete he was trying to lure to his school. The package was damaged in transport and as a matter of routine a representative of the delivery company made out a report noting the contents of the package, the sender and the intended receiver. Obviously the package contained an inducement that is illegal according to the rules of the National Collegiate Athletic Association. The media picked up the story and an investigation by the NCAA followed. The high school athlete, who never received the money and therefore had no direct blame in the case, was, by the established penalty system, permanently barred from playing at the University of Kentucky. This is a typical example of why coaches who break the rules are bad news for you.

Recruiting violations affect more than just the involved coach and athlete—they affect the entire athletic program at the college or university. Following the thousand-dollar incident at Kentucky, the University's basketball team was placed on probation and penalized (as explained below) by the NCAA. So an entire team of boys who had nothing to do with the incident found their college athletic careers and reputations damaged by a coach who thought he wouldn't get caught trying to hook a prize athlete who never even made it to the university.

Although each athletic association has established its own set of penalties, when athletic rules are broken the consequences are quite similar. Most often the involved athletic program is put on probation for a given number of years and/or required to abide by certain sanctions determined by the severity of the offense. Possible sanctions include:

- no postseason championships in the involved sport
- no TV coverage for the involved sport
- a reduction in the allowable number of scholarships given in the involved sport
- recruiting restrictions that could include the elimination of off-campus recruiting and/or official paid visits.

The effects of these penalties are longterm. Sanctions levied in an athlete's freshman year, for example, are felt most strongly two years later when over time the team has forfeited their recruiting advantage through lost scholarship money, recruiting restrictions and poor program reputation. The quality of the entire team is diminished when talented athletes stop enrolling in the school.

This penalty system, which in dragnet style swoops up the coaches, recruits and team members, gives you good reason to avoid completely any college or university that attempts illegal recruiting tactics. Coaches who are willing to bend rules for you, have surely done the same with other students in the past and will do it again in the future. (The odds are that at some point in your four years at college, blatantly unscrupulous coaches will bring down an entire athletic program.)

Consider this scenario: You sign a National Letter of Intent with a university that, unknown to you, is currently under investigation for rule infractions. Two years later the coach is found guilty leaving you to finish out your athletic career in a sanctioned program. Richard Hilliard, NCAA Director of Enforcement, suggests that you can avoid this kind of situation by asking every college coach who recruits you these four questions:

1. Has your program or institution ever been on probation for breaking the rules of your athletic association?
2. Have you ever been involved in a rules infraction investigation?
3. Have you ever been found in violation of an association regulation?
4. Is your program currently being investigated?

These are not unreasonable questions considering the frequency with which rules are broken. The NCAA processes about 20 major and 400 secondary new infraction cases every year, while the National Association of Intercollegiate Athletics (the second largest U.S. athletic association) processes about 125 violations every year.

Another, and equally important, strategy for avoiding rule violation problems in the recruiting process is to know the rules yourself. Even before the recruiters come knocking, you should make a pledge to learn and abide by the rules of the athletic associations.

ATHLETIC ASSOCIATIONS

Each athletic association has its own eligibility requirements. No one has them all memorized, but every coach has a copy of them and you should too. As soon as a coach or recruiter contacts you, ask for a printed copy of recruiting and eligibility rules. You can often learn something about coaches' ethics by noting the response. A beat-around-the-bush or never-deliver reaction can spell trouble. Be insistent and in the meantime contact the association for your own copy.

There are three associations that govern the majority of college and university athletic programs: The National Collegiate Athletic Association (NCAA), the National Association of Intercollegiate Athletics (NAIA) and the National Junior College Athletic Association (NJCAA). This chapter will outline the eligibility and recruiting rules that are most commonly encountered by young athletes interested in attending NCAA and NAIA schools. (The rules of the NJCAA are discussed in Chapter Ten.)

The information in this chapter has been obtained from official association publications and from interviews with an NCAA legislative assistant, the NCAA Director of Enforcement and the NAIA Director of Administrative Services. These representatives have reviewed the chapter just prior to publication in 1993 and have found the information to be accurate and up to date at that time. However, because the rules and regulations can change from year to year, be sure to get the most recent rule books from the appropriate association.

As you read the academic eligibility rules, keep in mind that they are the minimum requirements of collegiate athletic participation. Your high school graduation requirements may be more stringent and the college or university may have admission requirements that supercede the athletic requirements. Be sure to discuss high school graduation requirements with your guidance counselor and obtain admission requirement information from each college you want to apply to.

The National Collegiate Athletic Association (NCAA)

The National Collegiate Athletic Association is an organization of over 500 member colleges that makes rules governing eligibility, recruiting and financial aid. It has established these regulations in the following sports: men's and women's basketball, fencing, golf, gymnastics, lacrosse, rifle, skiing, swimming, track and field and volleyball; men's baseball, football, ice hockey, water polo and wrestling; and women's softball.

Athletic regulations can vary among Division I, II and III schools and so where necessary the Division differences have been noted in the following sections.

NCAA ACADEMIC ELIGIBILITY REQUIREMENTS

If you want to practice and play your freshman year at an NCAA Division I or Division II college, you must satisfy the requirements of the NCAA Bylaw 14.3, commonly known as Proposition 48. This bylaw requires you to:

1. graduate from high school.
2. attain a grade-point average of 2.000 (based on a maximum of 4.000) in a successfully completed core curriculum of at least 11 academic courses. (Successful completion is defined as a nonfailing grade of "D" or above.)
3. achieve a 700 combined score on the SAT verbal and math sections or an 18 composite score on the ACT.

The grade values are based on this equation:

A = 4 quality points
B = 3 quality points
C = 2 quality points
D = 1 quality point

A school's normal practice of weighting honors or advanced courses may be used to compute the quality points awarded in those courses and the accumulative grade-point average, provided a written statement verifying the grading policy accompanies your official grade transcript.

The 11 courses in the core curriculum must meet these criteria:

1. The 11 courses must include at least three years in English, two in mathematics, two in social science, and two in natural or

physical science (including at least one laboratory class if offered by the high school).

2. The two remaining units of additional academic credit must be from courses in the above areas or in foreign language, computer science, philosophy or nondoctrinal religion (e.g., comparative religion) courses.

3. Courses that are taught at a level below the high school's regular academic instructional level (e.g., remedial, special education or compensatory) cannot be considered core courses regardless of the course content.

   High school courses for the learning disabled or handicapped may be used to meet the core-course requirement if the high school principal submits a written statement to the NCAA indicating that students in such courses are expected to acquire the same knowledge, quantitatively and qualitatively, as students in other core courses and that the same grading standards are employed in such courses as those utilized in other core courses.

4. The core-curriculum grade-point average may be calculated using the student's 11 best grades from courses that meet the distribution requirements of the core curriculum. Additional core courses (beyond the 11 required) may be used to meet the core-curriculum grade-point average provided the distribution requirements are met.

5. Independent study or correspondence courses may not be used to satisfy the core-curriculum requirements.

6. Courses that are graded on a pass-fail basis may not be used to satisfy the core-curriculum requirements.

7. A one-year course that is spread over two years (e.g., elementary algebra) is considered as one course.

The following interpretations apply to the combination of test scores from more than one national testing date:

1. For students utilizing the SAT, the highest scores achieved on the verbal and mathematics section of the SAT from two different national testing dates may be combined in determin-

ing whether the student has met the minimum test-score requirement.

2. For students utilizing the ACT, the highest scores achieved on the individual subtests of the ACT from more than one national testing date may be combined in determining whether the student's composite score has met the minimum test-score requirements.

3. Prospects whose combined composite test score from more than one ACT results in a fraction (e.g., 17.5, 17.2) may round up from a minimum of .5 to the next whole number (e.g., 17.5 is changed to 18.0, but 17.2 is counted as 17.0).

The NCAA academic eligibility requirements will change on August 1, 1995. At that time all athletes must attain a grade-point average of 2.5 (an increase of .5 over the current requirement) in a core curriculum of at least 13 (an increase of 2) academic courses. These stricter requirements will be accompanied by a form of indexing that, for example, will allow an athlete who scores well above the minimum required 700 SAT score to be eligible even if his or her GPA is only 2.0. In the same way, the athlete with an above-minimum GPA will be eligible even with a 650 SAT.

Athletes who do not meet the NCAA academic eligibility requirements find themselves severely disadvantaged in the recruiting and college admissions arena. First, their scholarship and institutional financial aid possibilities are affected as explained in Chapter Eight. In addition, ineligible athletes cannot participate in intercollegiate athletics for one year at the college in which they enroll. If after one year they meet the collegiate academic requirements, they may then participate in athletics. Athletes who are ineligible as freshmen at Division I schools lose that year of athletic eligibility and can then participate in a collegiate sport for only three years. Athletes who are ineligible as freshmen at Division II schools do not lose a year of athletic eligibility and if eligible in their sophomore year can participate for the full four years.

The NCAA does not set academic eligibility regulations for Division III schools. Each prospective athlete must meet the eligibility requirements of the college or university itself. If students are eligible for admission, they are eligible for athletics.

NCAA RECRUITING REGULATIONS

College coaches and recruiters are restricted by NCAA rules in the kind, number and place of contacts they can make with high school athletes. The NCAA defines *contact* as any face-to-face meeting between a college coach and an athlete or an athlete's parents during which anyone says more than "hello." Furthermore, any face-to-face meeting that is prearranged, or occurs at a high school or at any competition or practice site is a contact, regardless of the conversation.

Contact Restrictions: In all NCAA Divisions, letters from coaches, faculty members and students are not permitted until September 1 at the beginning of the athlete's junior year in high school. College coaches and faculty members may contact an athlete by telephone or in person off the campus only on or after July 1 following the completion of the junior year. These rules make it clear that college coaches cannot correspond or meet with high school freshmen or sophomores. If a coach drops by to say "Hi" to you in your sophomore year, he isn't being friendly; he's trying to get a recruiting advantage and is jeopardizing your athletic eligibility.

In all Division I and II sports coaches may contact senior-year athletes at any site *off-campus* a total of three times. But at your own expense, you can have *on-campus* visits any time. On such a visit, you may receive a maximum of three complimentary admissions for yourself and those who accompany you to a game on that campus and a tour of off-campus practice and competition sites in your sport and other institutional facilities within 30 miles of the campus.

During your senior year in high school, you may receive only one expense-paid (official) visit to a particular campus and you may receive no more than five such visits to Division I or II schools. This restriction applies even if you are being recruited in more than one sport. During the official visit (which cannot exceed 48 hours), you may receive round-trip transportation between home and campus. During this visit, you and your parents may receive meals, lodging and complimentary admissions to campus athletics events. In addition, a student host may help you and your family become acquainted with campus life. The host may be given $20 per day to cover all costs of entertaining; however, the money cannot be used to purchase college souvenirs such as T- shirts or other college mementos.

Effective August 1, 1992, a college may not provide an official visit unless the athlete has presented the college with a PSAT, SAT or ACT score taken on a national test date under national testing conditions.

The rules of contact in Division III schools are the same as those in Division I and II schools with these exceptions:

- There is no limit on the number of contacts a coach may make or when such contacts may occur.
- There is no limit on the number of campuses that an athlete may visit.
- A student does not have to supply PSAT, SAT or ACT scores before the official visit.

Whether you are applying to Division I, II or III schools remember this simple but most important rule of recruiting: An athlete or members of the athlete's family may not receive any benefit, inducement or arrangement such as cash, clothing, cars, improper expenses, transportation, gifts or loans to encourage the athlete to sign a National Letter of Intent or to attend an NCAA school. Fancy dinners, elaborate gifts and cash are tempting offers that can be difficult to turn down. But the tales of the many young athletes, like the basketball player whose thousand-dollar gift was intercepted in the mail, who have suffered because unscrupulous coaches break the rules should forewarn you about the irreversible consequences.

Evaluation Periods: An evaluation is any off-campus activity designed to assess an athlete's academic qualifications or athletics ability, including any visit to a high school or the observation of any practice or competition at any site at which athletes participate.

In all Division I and II sports coaches may evaluate an athlete on not more than four occasions during the academic year. All competition that occurs on consecutive days within a tournament and (normally at the same site) or that involves a tier of a tournament counts as a single evaluation.

In the sports of football and basketball there are additional restrictions on when a coach may contact a high school athlete off the college campus and/or attend practices and games to evaluate athletic ability. These contact and evaluation periods vary from sport to sport and from Division I to Division II. Each evaluation period is clearly listed in the NCAA student booklet available from the NCAA. (See Appendix for their address.) If you are involved in any of these sports, be sure you have these periods memorized or you may pay the same price paid by a young basketball player in 1985.

In 1984–85, Tito Horford was a heavily recruited basketball player who signed a Letter of Intent to attend the University of Houston. But before Horford made it to his first practice, it was discovered that a UH assistant coach had visited Tito during a period of time in which coaches were not allowed to have in-person contact with high school recruits. Because of this rule, which Horford was probably not even aware of, he was declared ineligible to play on the UH basketball team.

There are no restrictions on the number of contacts or period of time for evaluation of prospective Division III athletes.

TRYOUTS

According to NCAA rules, a tryout is any physical activity (e.g., practice session or test) conducted by a college, or arranged on behalf of the college, at which an athlete reveals, demonstrates, or displays ability.

High school athletes may NOT try out for Division I and Division III athletic teams.

High school athletes may try out for Division II college teams before enrollment provided it is done with the permission of the high school director of athletics. The tryout must occur after the completion of high school eligibility and may include tests to evaluate strength, speed, agility and sports skills. Except in the sports of football, ice hockey, lacrosse, soccer and wrestling, the tryout may include competition.

NCAA AMATEUR STATUS REGULATIONS

In June 1991 the Yankees chose high school senior Brien Taylor as their No. 1 draft pick. Speaking through an "advisor" (known pro agent Scott Boras), Taylor told the media and the Yankees that he would not consider the Yankee's offer—reportedly worth $350,000; he wanted a $1.2 million dollar deal over three years.

By NCAA rules, Taylor became ineligible for collegiate competition as soon as he hired an agent and then again when he declined the first offer and asked for more money. Professional agents and contract negotiations of any kind are not allowed. If, for example, a recruit is offered $500,000 to compete in a professional sport, the athlete may say only "Yes" or "No." If the answer is "No" and the pro representative comes back a day later and says, "How about $700,000?" and the athlete says "Okay" there's no turning back. He or she has negotiated a deal; if the contract falls through or the athlete later decides college would be a better choice, the doors to intercollegiate competition at NCAA schools are closed.

Taylor and the Yankees bargained back and forth until the last possible moment. The press commented that the Yankees probably felt they had the negotiating advantage when Taylor threw away his back-up option of going to a four-year college. But then less than 12 hours before the young pitcher was to start classes at a junior college (where he could still play baseball and where the Yankees would not have been able to talk to him until after his baseball season), he accepted the Yankees' improved offer. The move was probably a smart one because it's unlikely that Taylor would have ever earned a bachelor's degree since he could never transfer into a four-year college and earn a diploma while playing baseball—those doors were shut.

Most amateur status rules pertain to college athletes, but the ones above and the following four apply directly to high school athletes:

A student-athlete SHALL NOT be eligible in a Division I, II or III sport if the student has:

1. Ever taken pay, or accepted the promise of pay, in any form, for participation in that sport.

2. Ever entered into an agreement of any kind to compete in professional athletics in that sport, or to negotiate a professional contract in that sport.

3. Ever directly or indirectly used athletic skill for pay in any form in that sport.

4. Ever signed a contract or commitment of any kind, regardless of its legal enforceability or the consideration (if any) received, to play professional athletics in that sport.

High school athletes (even those who have signed a Letter of Intent with an NCAA institution) *may* try out for a professional sports organization without jeopardizing their eligibility. Once they become enrolled in a college by attending the first day of classes, however, they can no longer try out for professional teams without forfeiting their collegiate eligibility.

After enrollment in college, NCAA athletes cannot accept money or gifts for the use of their name or image in commercial publications and they may not endorse or promote commercial products or services. Without a clear understanding of this rule it can easily and innocently be broken—even in the publication of this book. If I, for example, interviewed an athlete about her recruiting experience and then sent money or a gift to say thanks for the interview, the gesture would be a violation of NCAA rules. Or, if an advertising agent for the publisher took an athlete's quoted remark from this book and put it on a sales flyer, the athlete would be involved in a commercial promotion—unknowingly and unwillingly, but involved just the same. That's why each athlete presented in this book has been given a pseudonym to protect his or her intercollegiate eligibility.

NCAA REGULATIONS FOR UNOFFICIAL RECRUITERS

Although college coaches and high school athletes are the primary players in the recruiting game, there are other secondary players who must also abide by the rules. Unfortunately, because their jobs and/or college careers aren't jeopardized by bending the rules and because they often don't know the rules, they can come between you and your goals. The unofficial recruiters you should watch out for are unprincipled or uninformed high school coaches and overly ambitious college boosters. Consider these two scenarios:

A high school coach offers to take one of his athletes to visit a nearby college. During the visit they stop by to talk with the college coach. The college coach invites the teen and his coach out to lunch; the college coach picks up the tab and gives the high school coach a $20 bill to pay for the day's gas and tolls. They all say goodbye, shake hands, and the teen and his coach consider the visit a very productive one.

On another day a neatly dressed young man approaches this same young athlete after a local competition to congratulate him on a superb performance. He suggests that the teen might consider playing at his alma mater and invites the boy and his parents out for a bite to eat to talk about the college and its opportunities.

Both situations seem innocent enough, but both are in direct violation of NCAA recruiting rules and could cause this athlete to forfeit his eligibility at these two colleges. Because not all coaches and boosters know or care about the rules of recruiting, you must know them and avoid anyone who suggests they can be broken.

Rules for High School Coaches: Although the majority of coaches are honorable people who would never intentionally hurt the collegiate careers of their athletes, they are not always aware that the rules apply to them too. The rules that most directly affect high school coaches state that a university representative may not:

1. pay back a high school coach for the costs of transporting an athlete to visit the campus, or
2. entertain a high school coach at any location except on the college campus, or in the community where the college is located. The university cannot pay for the coach's food and refreshments, room expenses or the cost of transportation to and from the campus. Permissible entertainment for a high school coach is limited to two tickets to an athletic contest.

Rules for Boosters: A booster is any person who represents an institution's athletic interests; most commonly this is an alumnus or college sport fan. Boosters serve a positive role in collegiate athletics because many financially support athletic programs, scholarship funds and even coaches' salaries. It's estimated that the average NCAA Division I college gets about $300,000 each year from boosters. Certainly colleges need boosters.

However, some boosters will do anything to be involved in the making of championship teams. They blatantly disregard NCAA recruiting rules without concern because they are not officially connected to the college and can't be penalized for infractions. But the athletes they lure outside the established recruiting process will bear the same penalties imposed when the rule infractions are committed by themselves or by college or high school coaches.

Because overly-enthusiastic boosters have for years plagued the legitimate recruiting efforts of college coaches, the NCAA has established very clear recruiting rules for boosters. Many boosters ignore them, so make sure you know them.

Division I Rules Regarding Boosters: Boosters cannot be involved in any way in the recruiting process. They may make no contact with potential athletes, their legal guardians or their relatives. This includes off-campus, on-campus, in person, by telephone or by mail contacts. NO contact is allowed.

Division II Rules Regarding Boosters: Boosters cannot make any in-person, off-campus recruiting contacts. They may, however, meet with an athlete on the college campus and they may correspond by phone or mail.

Division III Rules Regarding Boosters: Boosters cannot contact young athletes until after their junior year of high school. After this time there are no restrictions on the form, location or number of contacts that boosters can make.

The National Association of Intercollegiate Athletics (NAIA)

The National Association of Intercollegiate Athletics (NAIA) is an organization of approximately 425 four-year colleges and universities. It organizes and administers all areas of intercollegiate athletics for its member schools at the national level including rules and standards, and district and national competitions. Individual institutions and/or conferences can name stricter regulations than the national rules (in any area), but can never be more lenient. The NAIA offers national championships in men's and women's cross country, soccer, indoor and outdoor track and field, swimming and diving, basketball and tennis; in men's football, wrestling, baseball and golf; and in women's volleyball and softball.

NAIA ACADEMIC ELIGIBILITY REQUIREMENTS

Students who wish to compete during their freshman year at an NAIA institution must graduate from an accredited high school and be accepted for admission by an NAIA member school. In addition, to be eligible to represent a member institution in any manner, a first-time entering freshman must meet two of three entry level requirements:

1. Obtain a score of 18 on the ACT or a score of 740 on the SAT (scores must be achieved on a single test),
2. achieve an overall high school grade-point average of 2.000 on a 4.000 scale, or
3. graduate in the top half of the high school graduating class.

Athletes who do not meet the NAIA eligibility requirements may not represent the institution in intercollegiate competition for the first two semesters or three quarters of the student's enrollment in school. However, they can still receive athletic scholarship money if the school chooses to award it. Ineligible athletes can still practice with the team but they can't enter into any intercollegiate competition (including scrimmages and junior varsity play). These athletes do not lose a year of athletic eligibility; after their freshman year they can play for another four seasons.

NAIA RECRUITING REGULATIONS

Unlike the college coaches and recruiters in the NCAA, athletic representatives of the NAIA generally are not restricted in the number or kind of recruiting contacts they can make with high school athletes.

On-campus official visits for which athletes are reimbursed transportation costs and are offered meals or lodging are permissible under certain conditions. If such visits are part of the institution's existing policy regarding the recruitment of other talented students, then athletes too can be offered the same accommodations. If, for example, the college invites and entertains potential band members, then it can also invite and entertain (in the same manner) potential athletes. But under no conditions may an individual or organization provide direct financial assistance to a previously enrolled or prospective student.

Like the NCAA, NAIA rules and regulations absolutely prohibit the use of any form of remuneration either in money or gifts as recruiting incentives.

Evaluation Periods: Coaches at NAIA institutions can contact athletes of any age and grade and do not have specified contact or evaluation periods for any sport. Recruiters may meet with athletes and evaluate their athletic skills at any opportunity. If, however, a high school representative, a high school activities association or an athlete should ask recruiters to limit the number, location or timing of these contacts, the recruiter is bound by NAIA codes of ethics to do so.

Tryouts: High school athletes may be asked by NAIA institutions to try out for an athletic team under certain conditions. The tryout must be held on campus; it cannot involve any loss of school time; and it has to be a part of the institution's overall policy for recruiting any student with special ability. So if the school allows prospective choir members to audition, they can also allow athletic coaches to require a tryout.

NAIA AMATEUR STATUS REGULATIONS

By negotiating his pro opportunities, Yankee draft choice Brien Taylor closed the doors not only to NCAA schools but to NAIA schools as well. The amateur status regulations regarding commercial agents and contract negotiations are the same for both associations—they are not allowed.

To define the rule regarding amateurism NAIA Director of Administrative Services, Robert Rhoads, says very directly, "If an athlete has *ever* been paid to play or has negotiated an agreement to play, we consider him or her a professional and therefore ineligible for intercollegiate competition." In addition to receiving pay to play, and negotiating contracts, there are other ways an athlete can lose amateur standing. For example, a student will lose amateur standing in a sport by participating in an athletic contest as a professional or as a member of a professional team. This is interpreted to mean if anyone on the team is, by NAIA standards, considered a professional, then everyone on that team is considered a professional. (It should be noted that a student who loses amateur standing, loses standing only in the sport[s] involved.)

There is a process through which an institution may request reinstatement of amateur standing, on behalf of a student who has lost amateur standing in a sport. This process is detailed in Article VII, Section E of the NAIA bylaws.

NAIA REGULATIONS REGARDING UNOFFICIAL RECRUITERS

The NAIA does not prohibit athletic boosters from contacting high school recruits. However, boosters are bound by the same recruiting regulations that apply to any institutional representative: "Any remuneration, either in money or in kind, given to an athlete must come directly from the institution." This gives the school control over the funds the athletic department uses for recruiting purposes, and it makes it illegal for boosters to buy even a can of soda for a high school athlete.

BE SMART—BE SAFE

The rules and regulations that govern participation in intercollegiate athletics are many and complex. In this chapter I've explained only a few that commonly affect high school students who are recruited by two of the largest athletic associations. There are many more rules and other associations not even mentioned. (See the Appendix for the complete list of athletic associations.) In addition, each college, university and athletic conference may have regulations governing athletic participation that add to or supercede those of the association. The voluminous number of rules and regulations may seem too confusing to fully understand, but don't throw up your hands in confusion and decide with eyes closed to hope for the best. You've worked too long and too hard to let ignorance of rules that are designed to protect you turn around and discourage you. At the same time, it's not necessary to spend nights hunched over the rule books or to walk around paranoid that everyone who says "Nice game" is out to ruin your college athletic career.

Protect yourself in a reasonable and intelligent manner. Study the rules in this chapter; they are the ones almost always at the center of controversy in rule disputes. Then get an up-to-date rule book and refer to it whenever in doubt. And if the book can't clearly answer your questions, you can write to NCAA or NAIA for information.

College coaches are probably not the best source for eligibility interpretations. The majority are honest, hard-working people who do not knowingly break recruiting rules, but most are too busy coaching to keep up with every rule change every year. Your best bet is to contact the Faculty Athletics Representative at any NCAA or NAIA institution; these people are, by far, the personnel best informed regarding athletic rules and regulations. Throughout the preparation of this chapter, no one at any association was too busy to answer, look up, find out, or call me back about even the most minuscule detail of a rule.

Take the rules and regulations of athletic participation for what they are—a means of keeping the college experience an academic one, of protecting you from exploitation and of guaranteeing that amateur athletes don't unfairly compete against professionals.

C H A P T E R 6

TAKING A CAMPUS VISIT

Lorraine Taylor wanted to play college basketball. So the summer before her senior year she sent her athletic resume to 75 colleges that matched her academic goals. Between July and October she heard back from 28 of them. By December she had narrowed down the number and officially applied to her top four choices: Boston University, Lafayette College, Manhattan College and the University of Vermont. Coaches from all four schools offered her an official campus visit and she took them on four weekends in January. Thinking back now, Lorraine says, "On paper all four schools were just right for me, but now I know that you can't really be sure until you visit. Once I got to the campuses I got a feel for the people, the location and the school program. If I didn't visit the schools I'm sure I'd be in the wrong place now because my first choice school turned out to be a place where I wouldn't want to live."

Peter Orschiedt, undergraduate admissions officer at Cornell University (and a former college athlete himself) agrees with Lorraine's observations about the importance of the campus visit.

"When you go looking for a college," he says, "you're a consumer; you're shopping for the place where you're going to be most comfortable. The choice of one college over another often comes from a gut, personal feeling that you can get only by being there."

For prospective athletes who will need more information about coaches, athletics and sport facilities than is explained in the college catalogs, the visit becomes especially important. But before you run out and visit any campus you can get to—wait. A visit that is ill-timed or unorganized can be a confusing waste of time and energy. Campus visits are most productive when you take time to learn all you can about the school *before* you visit and when you go knowing there's a good chance you'll be admitted and make the team.

LEARNING MORE ABOUT THE COLLEGE

When a coach you've contacted expresses an interest in learning more about you, immediately contact the college's admissions department to learn more about the school. By phone or by mail ask for a college catalog, information about the subject field you're interested in and details about the school's athletic department (be sure you know the team's nickname and conference or league, their playing schedule and their win-loss record).

This information serves several purposes before a campus visit. First, it gives you more information to help narrow down the number of schools you'll actually visit. Second, it gives you facts about the school and athletic department that you can use in conversation with college coaches who are recruiting you. Third, it prepares you for successful admission interviews during your campus visit. And last, this knowledge keeps you from appearing as if you sent out hundreds of random applications in the hopes of landing just anywhere. Coaches and admission officers are more willing to give their time and attention to students who know something about the school and have applied for specific reasons.

When the college material starts to arrive, keep the information organized. A shoe box under the bed full of catalogs, papers, letters and pamphlets isn't very useful. Buy manila folders and as college material arrives put it in a folder labeled with the school's name. Then when a coach calls, you can grab the right folder and have instant access to information about the athletic and academic program.

You'll probably receive material from many colleges you didn't even contact. When you get a letter from an unsolicited school, size up its potential by using the Chapter Three worksheets. If the college meets your listed criteria start a folder for the school and send a resume to the coach.

At this point, where you and the coaches are just getting to know each other, there's no urgent need for a campus visit.

TIMING YOUR VISITS

The purpose of a college visit for student-athletes in their junior year of high school is very different from visits taken in the senior year. So as you plan your visits, keep in mind that timing has a lot to do with what you will get out of them.

Junior-Year Visits

Many students tour campuses during their junior year in high school. These campus visits help the students make the kind of decisions that are necessary to answer the worksheet questions in Chapter Three, which narrow down the number of schools the student will contact. It can resolve questions like: Do I like urban or rural campuses? Do I like large or small schools? Is the school too far away? Do I like the climate? These visits usually include a routine tour of the campus and a group question-and-answer session with an admissions officer. They are informative in a general way and can help students decide which schools they'd like to contact.

For most students hoping to participate in a college athletic program, however, the junior-year visit is premature. By association rules many college coaches can't meet with prospective athletes until *after* their junior year. Junior students also are usually ineligible for official campus visits that are arranged and paid for by the athletic department.

Still, if you'd like to make campus visits in your junior year, make them productive by following these suggestions:

1. Call ahead to find out when the campus tours are given.
2. Ask an admissions or athletic department representative for the phone number of a student who participates in your sport and call ahead to set up a meeting.
3. Be aggressive. Don't hesitiate to ask questions, eat the cafeteria food, go into the dormitories, and look at the locker rooms. Try to get beyond the limits of the guided tour.

Although junior-year visits can be a fun and informative way to begin the college selection process, it's the senior-year campus visits that are most focused and productive.

Senior-Year Visits

Student-athletes who have followed a timetable like the one suggested in this book know at the beginning of their senior year which schools are recruiting them and which ones they are academically qualified to attend. When you start to schedule campus visits, there should be no more than five to 10 schools on your list of possibilities (with at least two of these being back-up, safety schools where you know you'll be accepted). Under these circumstances the campus visit serves the very specific purpose of gathering first-hand information about the schools and athletic programs that are definitely in the running.

Senior-year visits can be taken either before or after you make formal application to the college. If you're having trouble narrowing down your list to the manageable few you'll actually apply to, campus visits early in the senior year may help you decide. If you know exactly which five to ten schools you'd like to attend, you can apply first and then spread your visits out over your senior year or even wait for acceptance notification and visit only those which accept you and offer a spot in their athletic program. (Of course if you apply for early admissions, your timetable is quite different, as explained in the next chapter.)

Regardless when you schedule your senior-year visits, they should be carefully organized to include meetings with the college coach, an admissions officer, a faculty member and a student-athlete. The following sections will help you make the most of these meetings. Also, at the end of each section, you'll find question-and-answer forms that you can copy and bring with you on each campus visit.

VISITING THE COLLEGE COACH

As a prospective athlete you'll certainly want to visit with the college coach. If you are being recruited for the athletic program, your visit may be at the coach's invitation. In this case the coach is your host and the one who arranges the details of the visit. Be sure to explain before you arrive that you want to meet with an admissions officer, a faculty member and a student-athlete. You'll get more out of your visit if the coach knows in advance what you want to do.

The campus visit is your chance to ask questions that will help you decide if this athletic program has the facilities, opportunities and philosophy that match what you're looking for. Although not all athletes feel comfortable sitting down in interview style with a pen and pad to ask questions and record answers, it's not a bad or silly idea. Explain to the coach that you have a few questions you'd like to ask and that you're going to jot down the answers so you don't forget or get them mixed up with information you've received from other coaches. To keep yourself organized, copy the question-and-answer form at the end of this section and write down the answers in the spaces provided. When it comes time to make your final decision and pick one school, you'll be glad you have these papers to look back on.

The questions on the form are just some of the questions you should ask a coach. The questions suggested in Chapter Five regarding NCAA or NAIA investigations and infractions should be asked before you get this far in the selection process; the questions that will help you make your final decision are listed in Chapter Nine, and if you have other questions you want to add to the list, write them on the back of the answer form after you make a copy from the book.

QUESTIONS FOR COACHES

School _____

Coach _____

Visitation date _____

1. How much time each week do the athletes on your team practice?_____
2. What is your typical travel schedule? _____
   _____
3. What off-season activities are your athletes expeced to participate in?
   _____
4. Are the athletic facilities adequate to handle the practice and competition schedules of all sports?_____
5. Can your athletes participate in another sport? _____
6. What is the average GPA of your athletes?_____
7. What percentage of your athletes graduate?_____
8. Are tutors available to athletes? _____
   b. If so, are they available for both scholarship and non-scholarship athletes? _____
9. Are athletes housed together or with non-athletes? _____
10. Do athletes eat in a separate dining facilities or with other students? _____
11. Is there any possibility that this sport may be dropped from the college athletic department? (It has happened!)
    _____

Be careful you don't turn off a coach with questions that show you don't know anything about the program. Don't ask, for example, "What kind of season are you having this year?" Instead, you'll make yourself a more desirable recruit if you can show your interest with comments like, "It must have been tough losing your two starting players to injuries in the beginning of the season but you've really pulled through. Do you think you'll be able to keep the winning streak going next season even though four of your top competitors are graduating?" This kind of question gives a coach the feeling that you want to participate in the program because you follow the team and root for their success and want to be a part of it—not just because you want to go anywhere someone will have you.

Once you've done your homework and learned all you can about the athletic program, don't be afraid to ask questions. As Lorraine Taylor told me, "The coaches want you to be happy if you decide to go to their college, so they don't mind if you ask questions and are usually honest with their answers."

VISITING AN ADMISSIONS OFFICER

Admissions officers are people employed by every college and university to help pave the way into college for high school students. They are trained to grab your interest, answer your questions and, if you meet their eligibility requirements, convince you to come to their school. You have to realize that to do these things they'll tell you only the good, positive and attractive stuff about their college, but they do have some facts you need before making your final college selection.

Try to schedule your guided tour before your admissions interview. The information you gain on the tour, along with what you've read in the catalog, will give you the details you need to ask intelligent questions. When I asked Peter Orschiedt of Cornell to suggest some questions a prospective student might ask an admissions officer, he joked about the student who comes in and asks, "Do you offer a major in business?" "I'm put off by that kind of question," Orschiedt says. "I'd much rather hear a student say something like, 'I've read that 11 percent of your students major in business and management. How are these programs structured?'" Once you've established that you've investigated your field of interest, you can go on to ask more specific and thoughtful questions like, "Are the majority of the classes held in lecture halls or smaller classrooms?" "Do graduate assistants or professors teach the freshman and sophomore classes?" "Do the courses have to be taken in a required order?" "What happens if the class is closed before I register?" "If I take summer courses at a college close to my home will the credits be accepted here?" These kinds of questions show you've taken the time to find out about the

QUESTIONS FOR ADMISSIONS OFFICERS

School _____

Officer _____

Date _____

1. The college catalog says the student/faculty ratio is _____.
   But in actual numbers, how many students are in an average
   class? _____
2. Are tutors available to undergraduates? _____
3. Does the faculty hold office hours? _____
4. Do the majority of full professors teach undergraduate
   courses or do graduate students teach the majority of
   freshman classes? _____
5. Are computers available to all students? _____
   b. During what hours? _____
   c. Is the college hooked up on a campus-wide data base?
   _____
6. Do you offer career counseling services? _____
7. Does the college have a career placement service that arranges
   for on- and off-campus job interviews? _____
8. Is there an intern program available during my off-season
   time? _____

institution and are interested in learning more than is explained in
the catalog.

Other questions you might ask are listed above. Remember to
write down the answers so you'll be able to compare schools when
it's time to make your final choice, and be sure to get the officer's
name so if you have more questions when you get home, you'll know
who to contact.

VISITING A FACULTY MEMBER

The coach and the admissions officer are informative, but biased,
members of the college staff. Faculty members, on the other hand, are
more likely to be truthful about the academic life of student-athletes.

It is the professors and instructors who know first-hand how athletes compare to the general student population in the academic arena. They also know how many students in your area of interest graduate in four years, how many must attend summer classes, how many fail lab courses because of their athletic schedule and how faculty/student relations are influenced by the athlete's schedule.

In addition to these points, most of the questions you'll want to ask a faculty member will depend on your major or field of interest so a comprehensive list cannot be provided for you to use on your interview. But the basic rules of questioning are the same: Before you visit the campus, study the college catalogs and make a list of questions that will lead you to *more* information. Also, be sure to review the curriculum guide before your interview so you don't embarrass yourself by asking silly, obvious or irrelevant questions.

VISITING A STUDENT-ATHLETE

If a college coach arranges your campus visit, it's most likely that you'll be paired with a student-athlete host. This person is your most valuable resource for finding out how enrolled students feel about everything from social life to academics. If the coach has arranged your visit, ask in advance for the opportunity to meet with a student-athlete. If you are organizing your own visit, call the athletic department beforehand and ask for a student-athlete guide.

Student-hosts can take you beyond the gym to the library, student center, cafeteria and dorms. They can take you to their classes; they can introduce you to fellow students. They can share their own recruiting experiences and introduce you to dorm life by letting you be their overnight guest.

The list of questions on the next page will give you an idea of the things student-athletes can tell you, but once you're on the campus, you'll think of lots more so be sure to copy the form in the book and use the back of the copy to jot down your own questions, observations and points of interest you want to remember.

QUESTIONS FOR STUDENT-ATHLETES

School _____

Student _____

Date _____

1. Are faculty members understanding when athletes have to miss classes because of their athletic schedule? _____
2. What kind of accommodations are provided for athletes when they travel to away competitions? _____
3. How would you describe the general student body? _____
   b. What is the overall attitude toward athletes? _____
4. Are you able to keep up with your class work during the sport season? _____
5. Do you have an academic advisor who helps you schedule your classes so you're not overburdened in-season, but still carry enough credits to remain eligible athletically? _____
6. Do many members of the team go to summer school? _____
7. How would you describe the coach? Is he or she knowledgeable? understanding? approachable? _____
8. Do the team members get along or do they fight among themselves? _____
9. Has the college lived up to your expectations? _____
10. Has anything about the school or athletic department surprised or disappointed you? _____

FOLLOWING THE RULES

Because you visit a college campus as a prospective athlete, you have to remember there are athletic association rules that govern these visits and can directly affect your eligibility.

NCAA Rules

If you hope to attend NCAA schools you should make your campus visits in your senior year for a number of reasons. As mentioned in Chapter Five, you cannot meet with college coaches on campus until after July 1 following your junior year and recruited senior-year students are allowed one expense-paid visit to a total of five NCAA schools. So because you'll certainly want to discuss athletics with the coach and take advantage of expense-paid visits, it makes sense to visit campuses in your senior year.

If you do plan to visit Division I, II or III schools be sure to review the rules of these visits explained in Chapter Five, talk with the college coach and read over the booklet, *NCAA Guide for the College-Bound Student-Athlete*, available from the NCAA at the address listed in the Appendix. Briefly, these rules include regulations that state:

- The college may pay for round-trip, coach-fare transportation between your home and the campus.
- Official visits can last no more than 48 hours.
- Students may be given tours of facilities only within a 30-mile radius of the campus.
- Students may receive meals, lodging and complimentary admissions to campus athletic events. (Such admissions may provide seating only in the general seating area of the facility used for the event. Special seating is prohibited.)

    You can visit any campus any time at your own expense. But still some rules apply:
- You may receive a maximum of three complimentary admissions to a game on that campus.
- A tour of off-campus practice and competition sites in your sport and other institutional facililties may not extend beyond 30 miles from the campus.
- You may receive a meal in the college's on-campus student dining facilities, and housing, provided it is available to all visiting prospective students.

NAIA Rules

The rules governing campus visitation of NAIA colleges vary from school to school. The association guidelines state that athletic recruiters can offer prospective students only the same opportunities offered by college policy to all visiting students. So because Lenoir-

Rhyne College in North Carolina routinely picks up visiting prospective students from the airport and feeds them on campus, the college's coaches can offer the same courtesy to their recruits. Also, no one from the institution can provide *direct* financial assistance to the athlete (i.e. the institution representative may purchase the plane ticket for the student, but may not send the money to the athlete). Although this guideline leaves some room for misunderstandings, you can generally assume that if an NAIA coach offers you first-class transportation, high-class restaurant meals, and overnight lodging in a luxury hotel, the visit is in violation of NAIA recruiting rules.

YOUR PARENTS AND THE INTERVIEW PROCESS

Parents have an important role to play during a campus visit so they are rarely left behind. Your parents, too, are anxious to get a feel for the place you may choose to spend your four years after high school. They are often good at offering support and keeping track of what you want to see and whom you want to talk to. They are not, however, the ones who must gather information and make the final decisions.

When you arrive for your scheduled meetings with a coach, administrator or faculty member, leave your parents at the door. Your interviews should be yours alone. Your parents won't be with you on campus once you're accepted, so it's a good idea to assert some independence and personal confidence during your interviews. When your interviews are finished, you should certainly say that your parents have accompanied you to the campus and are waiting outside to say "hello." Then bring your parents in and introduce them.

A WORD OF ADVICE

After her four college visitations, Lorraine Taylor chose Manhattan College where she is now successfully involved in academic and athletic endeavors. But looking back she can see how she could have gotten more out of her campus visits if she had been more assertive. "I let the coaches tell me where to go and what to do and who to see," she admits. "At some colleges I sat in on classes; at others, I didn't. Sometimes I met with someone from the admissions office; other times I didn't see anyone at all who represented the academic interests of the school. I'm sure I could have done whatever I wanted if I just spoke up and said what I wanted to do."

Don't leave yourself open to regrets about your campus visitations. Use the information in this chapter to help you learn everything you can about this place you may soon call home.

COMPILING AN APPLICATION PACKET

Y ears ago a friend of mine wanted to play softball at a local state college. The college coach had seen Pat play and encouraged her to apply to his school and then call the athletic department if she was accepted.

Pat was confident she'd be accepted because she had a solid academic record that easily met the admission requirements. Even as the filing deadline approached and her parents nagged her to complete the application, she didn't worry. She brought the completed forms to her guidance counselor a full two days before the due date and asked her counselor to fill in the School Report and mail the entire package directly to the college. Assuming her job was done she thought no more about admissions and spent the next few months concentrating on staying in shape for softball.

At the end of May Pat realized she had never heard back from the college so she asked her counselor to call and find out what happened. The counselor was shocked to find that the admissions department had no record of Pat's application. She was not accepted and was not allowed to submit another application at such a late date.

Angry and desperate, Pat quickly applied to a two-year community college that had no application deadline. Although the school didn't meet any of her academic or athletic needs, Pat enrolled in the hope that she could transfer to the state college at the end of the year.

A few months later, Pat's former English teacher was helping the guidance counselor clear old files out of his office. There, under one of the boxes, she found Pat's application—it had never been mailed. Obviously the guidance counselor was to blame for Pat's collegiate fiasco, but Pat, too, had to shoulder much of the responsibility. She waited until the last minute (a notoriously hectic time in the guidance department) and never went back to verify that the application was mailed. She never inquired why the college didn't acknowledge receipt of her application as promised in the application instructions, and she didn't apply to a back-up school. Pat learned the hard way that even recruited athletes have to pay close attention to the details of their admission application.

It's true that in the admissions process, some recruited athletes have an advantage over nonathletes because college coaches will often spend much time and energy convincing admissions officers to accept their selected athletes. But still, like all prospective students, the athlete has to submit an application packet that is complete, impressive and on time so that the admissions officer has factual academic information to add to the coach's request. Unfortunately, in the excitement of the recruiting frenzy, the ultimate importance of the admissions packet is often underestimated, and in extreme cases like Pat's, even ignored. Don't make this mistake. Although your thoughts and dreams may be focused on collegiate athletics, remember this: If you're not admitted to the college you can't participate in the sports program. Take full responsibility for every aspect of your college admissions application.

YOUR BEST SHOT

Compiling a college application is very much like putting together an account portfolio. A business executive who wants to win a new client must put together an impressive overview of what the company has successfully done for other clients in the past and then explain what the company can do to meet the unique needs of the prospective client in the future. Your goal in putting together a college application is similiar: You want to compile information that shows what you have done for your teachers and community in the past and then suggest what you can offer to the college's academic and social community in the future.

The business client and the admissions officer will receive many performance portfolios to choose from; content will certainly be used as a deciding factor but so will other more subjective components. Appearance of the application, for example, can affect your chances of being selected. Consider the business client: He or she would never choose the company who prepares a sloppy resume with erasures, cross-outs, omissions and illegible handwriting over one that presents a neat and carefully prepared one. Don't expect an admissions officer to act differently just because you're an athlete. The appearance of your college application creates a first impression that may be a final deciding factor in your acceptance or rejection; if you mess it up you may not get another chance.

Another subjective aspect of application preparation involves what can be called the "extras." The extra time, the extra care, the extra effort, the extra attention you put into an application is noticeable. Filling in the blanks isn't enough; it's just the beginning. Providing full and helpful information takes time and effort. A college admissions officer can tell whether you have hastily filled in the blanks just to get the job done, or whether you have taken the time to use every question, every space and every opportunity to introduce yourself and to share your feelings, goals and objectives, and your hopes and aspirations of being selected as a contributing member of the college's student body. If you want the *best* possible response to your application, be sure to give it your *best* shot.

The information in this chapter targets a part of the college admissions process for athletes that's usually the exclusive domain of the high school guidance department. Because I don't pretend to know everything about the ins and outs of college applications, I've asked several high school guidance counselors to help me prepare this information for you. Although they assure me the chapter is accurate and up to date, they also suggest that you consult with your own guidance counselor before applying to colleges; your counselors need to know what you're doing, and there may be additional in-school guidelines and procedures that you should follow.

SENDING FOR THE APPLICATION PACKET

In the early fall of your senior year you should have selected a limited number of schools you'd like to apply to. Your original, junior-year contact list may have had 50 to 100 colleges on it, but now considering how many coaches have responded, how many are showing an active interest, and given your additional catalog and visitation information it's time to cut the list down to a realistic number.

Five to ten schools are the maximum number you should apply to. College applications are a time-consuming process for everyone involved: Your guidance counselor and selected teachers have to write recommendations, transcripts and school profiles have to be prepared, and you have to put together a well-written and thoughtful essay for each one. Besides being time-consuming, sending numerous applications all over the country indicates that you haven't put enough thought into what you want to do and where you'd like to go. If you can't reduce your list of possible colleges by the beginning of your senior year, talk to your guidance counselor and go back to Chapter Three to review your initial college-selection criteria. Remember: You must apply to schools that meet all your needs, not just your athletic ones. (You should also keep in mind that you must submit a fee ranging from $15 to $50 dollars with each application; save yourself some money by applying only to schools that you seriously want to attend.)

Once you've narrowed your list, call or write the admissions department at each school and ask for an application.

STAYING ORGANIZED

While you're waiting for your applications to arrive, reorganize the folder system you started in Chapter Five. Back when you were calling colleges for information, I suggested that you put each school's literature in a folder labeled with the college's name. Now go through the folders of the schools you've decided to apply to and throw out unnecessary papers and pamphlets. As each application arrives put it right into its folder. Make copies of Worksheet 3, which is printed on page 105 and staple one to the cover of each folder. This worksheet will help you remember which applications have been passed on to the guidance department, which schools still need your standardized test scores and which teachers you've asked for recommendations. It will also help you keep track of important dates like the filing deadlines. Do yourself a favor and use this worksheet; it will become valuable later when you can't remember who still needs what.

THE STUDENT SECTION

When you get each application—read it! Don't just skim it; sit down without a pen in hand and read it from beginning to end. Read the instructions; read the fine print; read everything. You're bound to make mistakes if you rush into the form without reading it first. I saw a typical example of this problem just this week as I'm writing this chapter: A young athlete was filling out an application to Tufts University during his study hall. Looking over his shoulder I saw two sentences printed in fine print in the upper right corner of the first page—two sentences he had obviously overlooked. They read, "Pages 9, 10, 15, 16 should be removed as one unit by loosening center staples in application packet. Do not cut these pages apart." The student had carefully cut the pages out of the booklet. Don't hurt yourself by jumping in before you know where you're going. Slow down and read.

Once you know what you're supposed to do, make a copy of the entire application. Use the copy as a practice form. This is the place where you can figure out how you can best explain "the nature of your community activities" on a four-inch line. Practice how you can best fit your honors, awards and special recognition for extracurricular activities into little boxes that measure one-quarter inch by one-half inch. And simply give yourself a chance to rehearse what you want to say and how you want to say it.

The Common Application

The approach to filling out applications described above takes more time than a quick, once-over approach, but admissions officers all agree it's worth it in the end. The only way you might reduce the time spent composing different essays and neatly filling in applications forms is to use what's called the common application. More than 100 colleges in the U.S. have agreed that students may apply by completing one common application. All colleges participating in the common application agreement sign a statement that they do not discriminate against the students who send in the common application instead of the individual one. So when you request an application, you might ask if the college uses the common form. This will save you time. However, if your grades are not as high as you'd like them to be, the individual application may be a better choice because it usually gives you more opportunities for personal input.

The Essay

The essay is the dreaded ogre of college applicants. It probably pains you to even read this section. But you should try to look at it in a positive way—it's the only place in your packet where you can personalize your information. It's your chance to share your feelings, to reveal your unique qualities or even to emphasize your interest in athletics. It's no more than a short conversation that you would have with an admissions officer sitting at your kitchen table. If you look at it this way, you can relax and be yourself. You don't need to use the 10-dollar vocabulary words that you've never used before. You don't need to be formal; when you write your essay, just be honest and be yourself.

There are two kinds of essays on many applications. Some schools request several mini-essays. Here, on three or four lines, you're asked to respond to a question such as the one on Bucknells's application that asked, "Briefly discuss which of these activities (extracurricular and personal activities or work experience) has had the most meaning for you, and why." Mini-essays leave no room for unorganized rambling. These essays are included to test your ability to organize your thoughts and to present them clearly and concisely.

The other kind of essay is the longer personal statement. These essays give you your best opportunity to set your application apart from the thousands of others that are submitted with similar grades and scores. Here you can offer insights into your values and strengths, give autobiographical information about your plans for the future and a peek at the ways in which you feel you will be an asset to the college community.

When you begin your essay think carefully about the question and answer it creatively yet directly. This may sound like a contradiction in terms but it's not. By "creatively" I mean that you should avoid repeating the factual academic and extracurricular information that is already recorded on the application. Instead, use the essay to discuss your feelings and attitudes about these things. When King's College asked its applicants to describe why they should be accepted into the college, the admissions officers were not looking for a run-down of academic achievements; they already had that information. They wanted a more creative description of how King's College matched the applicant's personal goals and how the college community would benefit by having that person on campus.

By "directly" I mean quite simply that you must discuss the question asked. To answer the question on John Hopkins University's application that says, "Explain how a particular literary work has influenced you," you can't go off on a tangent about your recent European vacation or your most memorable athletic experience unless you can find some way to wrap these stories tightly around a literary work. No matter how interesting and well-written, if the essay doesn't respond to the question, no one will be impressed. Stick to the subject.

Don't put your essay on the application form right away. First, write a practice draft just to get down your ideas. Then revise it so it's organized and reads smoothly and coherently. Then go back and check the mechanics of spelling, punctuation and sentence structure. This is an academic institution you're applying to; make sure that your essay is academically sound.

Although the contents of the essay must be entirely your own, the final product should be proofread by your English teacher. To benefit from this critique follow these three guidelines:

- Give your teacher at least a week to look over the essay. If you hand it in second period and need it back fifth period, you can't expect thorough or thoughtful feedback.
- Don't give your teacher the only copy you have. Make another copy so that if the essay gets mixed up with book reports and becomes "lost" for a week you won't panic. As a general rule, never let the original out of your hands.
- Give the teacher a practice essay. Every year I hear English teachers complain that students hand them the final essay typed on the official college application and ask, "How's this?" Well, if it's awful, it's too late to do anything about it.

When you've gotten your teacher's stamp of approval on your essays, you can transfer them to the application. Here, again, carefully follow the directions. Some schools request that the essay be handwritten and fit in the space provided. Others offer you the option of typing on a separate sheet of paper. Unless a handwritten copy is specifically requested, always type your essays. To an admissions officer who reads hundreds of essays each day, reading even the neatest handwriting can be a laborious task.

When you have completed your part of the application make a copy of every page to put in your folder. Then send the original to the college. Be sure to sign the form, include the application fee and note the date on your folder worksheet. When your application is received by the admissions department they will send you a note acknowledging its receipt, and then it will be held until the college also receives the guidance department section and the teachers' recommendations.

THE GUIDANCE COUNSELOR SECTION

Your application packet will request information from your guidance counselor. Although the guidance department is responsible for supplying this information, it is your responsibility to make sure you hand in the proper forms, that you give your counselor at least two weeks notice before the material is due, and that you double-check with your counselor a few days before the deadline to be sure the guidance packet has been mailed.

The first form the counselor should receive is called the School Report. Most colleges include this form in the student's application packet. Read this over before you give it to your counselor. Often you have to fill in prelimary information such as your name, address and social security number and then pass it on. This report is then completed and put together with your school transcript, a student activity record (often part of the transcript) and sometimes a school profile that helps admissions officers get a clearer picture of your academic and community background.

The only document that you need to review personally before it leaves the guidance office and heads out to the college is your student transcript. The transcript is probably the most informative paper you'll send to a college so go over it carefully to be sure it is up to date and accurate. It is possible that a course you dropped two years ago is still recorded on your course list. Your newly elected position of team captain may never have made it to your student activities sheet, and the most recent SAT or ACT scores may have been entered incorrectly. Your transcript is probably put together throughout your high school years by a number of different people. Only you can be sure it represents you accurately.

When you're content that the transcript is correct, tell your guidance counselor when the application materials must be sent to the college and mark the date you submitted the forms to your counselor on your folder worksheet. Then it's time to tackle the last application requirement—the teacher recommendations.

TEACHER RECOMMENDATIONS

Each college you apply to will ask for at least one teacher recommendation. Often a form for this purpose is included right in the application packet.

There is a right way and a wrong way to get teacher recommendations. The wrong way is to put the form on your teacher's desk with a note that says, "Please mail this before January 1st." The right way requires a bit more input on your part, but the end result is worth it. When requesting recommendations follow these steps to ensure that your teachers give you a good word:

1. Always ask the teachers of your choice if they would be willing to write your college recommendation. Teachers who like you personally may still be hesitant to recommend your academic abilities in that particular subject; give them a chance to back out or you'll end up with a lukewarm reference.
2. Give your teachers the recommendation forms well before the deadline so they have plenty of time to write a thoughtful piece.
3. Supply the teacher with written instructions. Explain exactly what you need so you won't end up with a mere repetition of factual data that you've already put on your application. Explain that the colleges are looking for information about attributes like a student's maturity level, intellectual curiosity and willingness to work hard to achieve goals. The factors of perserverence, determination and loyalty that were important in your athletic recommendations are also important in your academic ones.
4. Give your teacher written background information. Include an unofficial transcript or a list of your student activities and special accomplishments. These things give teachers concrete information to draw on.

5. Include a stamped, addressed envelope along with the recommendation form.
6. Follow up a week later with a thank-you note.

The recommendations are sent to the college in an envelope separate from your application. The teachers may choose to show you what they've written, but they don't have to. According to the Family Educational Rights and Privacy Act of 1974 you have the right to see your admissions file at any school in which you eventually enroll. But you do not have this right at schools that reject your application or which you choose not to attend. Since you aren't guaranteed the right to preview the recommendations before they're sent to the college, be sure you choose your teachers carefully.

FROM START TO FINISH

In the early fall of his senior year Roy Hopkins, my baseball pitcher, sent out two college applications to schools that matched the criteria he listed on his Chapter Three worksheet and where the baseball coaches showed interest in recruiting him. He later applied to two more schools, but I thought a look at how Roy completed his first two applications might help you see how easy the process can be once you get organized.

The first week of September, Roy called Stoney Hill University and Beacon University and asked for admissions applications. While waiting for them to arrive, Roy stapled copies of Worksheet 3 onto the front of two folders and filled in the dates he requested the material. Then he called the Educational Testing Service and requested that his SAT scores be sent directly to these schools. (He didn't list them on his SAT form the day he took the tests so he had to make this separate request.) Then Roy noted on his worksheet that this work was done.

Two weeks later the applications arrived and the application process began. Roy skimmed over the material when he got home from school, but then he put it aside until later that night when he knew he'd have time to read through each one without being interrupted.

After a careful reading, Roy pulled out the School Report sections along the perforated lines. He filled in Section A with his name and address and put them aside to give to his guidance counselor the next day. Then he pulled out the Instructor's Report from both applications and put them in stamped envelopes that he addressed to each college.

The next morning (Tuesday) he made three stops before homeroom. He dropped off the School Report forms at the guidance office and submitted a request for two unofficial student transcripts; then he stopped by his math and chemistry teachers' rooms to ask if they would write his college recommendation. When they agreed, he promised to come back with all the information they'd need.

Later that day in English class, Roy asked his teacher if she would proofread his personal statement essays when he finished the rough drafts. He had two completely different topics to write about and knew he'd need some help. Stoney Hill asked him to explain why he was applying to the university, and Beacon wanted him to imagine what he would be doing in the year 2000. By pretending that each was a homework assignment that he had to do, Roy was able to have first drafts ready for his teacher by Friday.

Also on Friday, Roy gave a copy of his transcript to his math and chemistry teachers along with his written instructions and the recommendation form in stamped envelopes.

Before leaving school that day, Roy made a copy of his applications so he could practice filling them out over the weekend. The applications weren't difficult to complete, but Roy did make a few mistakes filling in coded material from one section to another. He also needed the practice sheets to give him room to figure out the neatest way to fit the requested information in the little spaces provided. Sunday night Roy copied the data from the practice copies to the official forms and was finished with the fill-in-the-blanks part of the applications.

On Wednesday, Roy stayed after school for 15 minutes with his English teacher. She had corrected the mechanics of his essays and made a few suggestions about adding concrete examples to support some vague and abstract statements he had made. That night Roy made the suggested changes and wrote the essays over again. He had to make sure that they were legible because his mom had offered to type the compositions on her word processor at work if he had them ready for her on Friday morning.

On Saturday, Roy went to the library to make copies of his completed applications. Then he went to the post office and mailed them out. He went home and marked the date on his worksheet and he was finished! On Monday he gave his English, math and chemistry teachers thank-you notes. (He was saving the one he had for his guidance counselor until he had finished applying to his two other choices.)

All went very smoothly and quickly for Roy and still it took one month from the time he requested the applications to the time he mailed them in. And still he had two more applications to complete. Don't let yourself get caught short on time. Poor timing when contacting a college coach can reduce your chances of being recruited, but poor timing when submitting admissions applications can knock you out of the game completely.

TIMING

The time of year you apply to colleges depends on the kind of admission status you want. The following terms and their definitions will help you know when to get going on the application process.

Early Decision

Early decision is a plan of admissions in which the student applies at the end of the junior year or very early in the senior year and the college agrees to notify applicants of acceptance or rejection in the first semester of the senior year.

There are two types of early decision plans:

The Single-Choice Plan: In the single-choice plan students cannot apply to other colleges until they have received notification of rejection by the early decision college.

The First-Choice Plan: In the first-choice plan students can apply to other colleges, but they must name the early decision college as the first choice and agree to enroll at that college and withdraw all other applications if accepted.

If you want to apply to a college under an early decision plan you'll need to plan ahead. You have to complete all your required admission testing as soon as possible in your senior year, request an application at the end of your junior year and return it before the early deadline, which is generally sometime between October 15 and November 15.

The early decision plan is recommended only for athletes who are above-average academically, know exactly where they want to go to college and have been guaranteed, in writing before the beginning of the senior year, a spot on the college team. Because most students and coaches can't make this kind of early commitment, the majority of athletes apply under one of the other admission plans.

Early Action

Early action is a plan often confused with early decision, but it is quite different. Early action has the same early time frame as early decision, but it is not a binding commitment. If accepted, the early action student is promised admission by the college but does not have to withdraw other college applications or promise to attend that college.

If the colleges you're applying to offer the early action plan, it's a good, non-binding way of giving yourself peace of mind in your senior year. You'll know early if you can attend the college of your choice or if you need to keep applying elsewhere.

Early Evaluation

Early evaluation is a procedure used by Ivy League schools (Brown, Columbia, Cornell, Dartmouth, Harvard, Pennsylvania, Princeton and Yale) and the Massachusetts Institute of Technology. Under this plan, between November 1 and February 15 applicants can receive an evaluation of their chances for acceptance. Categories used are likely, possible, unlikely and insufficient evidence for evaluation. Final notification is made sometime in April.

Rolling Admissions

Rolling admissions is the practice of selecting students for admission as their completed applications are received. Schools who use this plan usually notify the applicants as soon as a decision is made and request a deposit to hold a place in the class.

It's important to know if a school uses a rolling admissions plan because timing then becomes a most important factor. The earlier you get in your application, the better your chances of being accepted.

Regular Admission

Regular admission is the process most students use to apply to colleges. This plan requires that you submit your completed application by a given date listed in the college catalog (most frequently sometime between January 1 and February 1). You'll be notified of acceptance or rejection by mail between mid-March and mid-April.

Whichever plan you choose, the best bet is to return the application EARLY. An early return shows you have a keen interest in the college and it allows your application to receive closer consideration. At the deadline, admissions officers are swamped with thousands of applications that can hardly get a thorough reading. You can make yours stand out by sending it in early.

If you don't get your applications mailed out early, be sure you understand what each college means by "deadline." Some schools want your application postmarked on that day; others want the application in their admissions office by that day. Such a slight difference of definition can make a world of difference if you try to slip in under the wire.

THE SENIOR SLIDE

The hours spent gathering information, filling out applications and writing essays are well rewarded when you receive a letter of acceptance from the college of your choice. But the road between when you mail in your application and when you graduate is not the easy

WORKSHEET # 3

APPLICATION CHECKLIST

COLLEGE: _____

application requested	_____	date:	_____
standardized test scores sent to college	_____	date:	_____
guidance information requested	_____	date:	_____
teacher recommendations distrubuted	_____	date:	_____
application deadline	_____	date:	_____
application mailed	_____	date:	_____
acknowledgement of receipt	_____	date:	_____

street some seniors think it is. Because the college coach has already evaluated your athletic abilities and the admissions officers have all the academic information they'll use to make their decision, right after you mail your applications probably seems like a good time to take it easy—but it isn't.

Your past athletic performances have made you a desirable prospective member of a college team. But it's your future performances that will determine if you compete in key positions or as a starter, and even if you stay on the team and/or keep your scholarship. So it's your responsibility to stay in shape. Work out, watch your diet and avoid injury.

Your academic record and the impressive quality of your application will certainly convince some admissions officers to admit you to their college. But the day you mail in your application package doesn't mark the end of your academic efforts. The "senior slide," as it's called is based on the mistaken belief that once your school records are in the hands of the admissions officers, you're home free. But don't forget that "Midyear Report" that was included in the guidance section of the application. Each college requires a midyear review of your grades before they make their final decision. (Even early decision and early action candidates are reviewed again midyear.)

Even after you're officially accepted by a college you're still not quite "in." When you sign your letter of acceptance, you enter into a contract with the college by which you agree to complete your senior year at the same level of achievement at which you originally applied. All colleges take second-half senior grades as a clear indication of a student's character and work ethic. They require high schools to send a final transcript for every admitted student. If these reports show a change from "A"s and "B"s to "C"s and "D"s, it is apparent that the student broke the acceptance contract and the college will move to find out why. Many colleges call the student's guidance counselor; others send letters to the school and the student's parents. Most require a written letter of explanation from the student. If there is reason for the change, such as a family death or divorce, the college will sympathize but may require the student to attend summer school. If there is no reasonable cause for the slide, the college can withdraw their offer of admission.

You've worked hard to find a good match between your athletic abilities and academic record. Once the match is sealed by the final acceptance into college, don't blow the whole deal by acting like you've got it made. What you've got is a responsibility to keep up the good work.

The National Association of College Admission Counselors has put together a list of student rights and responsibilities. I'll end this chapter by listing them below as a reminder that there's plenty of information available to you if you look for it, but it's your responsibility to make sure that what happened to my friend Pat never happens to you.

STATEMENT OF STUDENTS' RIGHTS AND RESPONSIBILITIES IN THE COLLEGE ADMISSIONS PROCESS

As a student applying to colleges and universities, you have both rights and responsibilities.

Your Rights Entitle You To:

- Receive full information from colleges and universities about their admission, financial aid, scholarship and housing policies. If you consider early decision application, obtain complete information from the college about its process and policy.
- Wait to respond to an offer of admission and/or financial aid until you have heard from all the colleges and universities to which you have applied or until May 1, whichever comes earlier.

If you think that your rights as a student have been denied, you should contact the college or university immediately to request additional information or the extension of a reply date. In addition, you should ask your counselor to notify the president of your state or regional Association of College Admission Counselors.

Your Responsibilities Are To:

- Understand the admission, financial aid and scholarship policies of the colleges and universities to which you plan to apply. This includes being aware of deadlines, restrictions and other criteria.
- Complete all material that is required for application, and submit your application materials on or before the deadlines.
- Follow the process recommended by your high school for filing college applications.
- Arrange, if appropriate, for interviews and/or visits to colleges of your choice.
- Notify each college or university that accepts you whether you are accepting or rejecting its offer. You should make these notifications as soon as you have heard from all the colleges to which you have applied or by May 1, whichever is earlier. Also, if you are accepted under an early decision plan, which requires you to attend that institution, you must withdraw the applications submitted to other colleges or universities at the time of that acceptance and make no additional applications. If you are an early decision candidate and are seeking financial aid, the previously mentioned withdrawal of other applications presumes you have received notification about financial aid.
- Confirm your intention to enroll and submit a deposit, if one is required, to only one college or university by its required notification date, usually May 1.

If you are put on a waiting list by a college or university and are later admitted by that institution, you may accept the offer and send a deposit. However, you must immediately notify any other college or university where you previously indicated your intention to enroll.

FINDING
FINANCIAL AID

Wendy Dorkin is playing volleyball at a state university. Her athletic scholarship is paying 50 percent of the $8,783 bill.

Wayne Chet is playing football at a large western university. His financial aid package is paying $14,672 of the $20,598 bill.

Jennifer Thompson is running track at a small private college in the south. Her athletic scholarship is paying the entire $6,300 bill.

Jose Lopez is wrestling at a selective private university. His athletic scholarship is paying $8,000; his local PTO scholarship is paying $500; his State Scholar Award is paying $1,000, and he is on a college work-study program earning $1,000. His family will pay the $3,650 balance.

As you can see, financial aid comes in all shapes and sizes. However, unless you're a highly recruited athlete, you'll have to go looking for the money to finance your college education; it will not come to you.

Look first to the college athletic departments where coaches have responded to your initial contact letters. As soon as you have mailed your applications to these colleges, write a letter to the coach telling him or her that you have officially applied to the school and now wonder what sources of financial aid are available to athletes in your sport. Because you've applied to the college, the coaches know that it wouldn't be a waste of their time to consider offering you an athletic scholarship or to steer you to other avenues of financial assistance.

While you're waiting for a reply, take some time to think about the pros and cons of athletic scholarships.

THE PROS AND CONS OF ATHLETIC SCHOLARSHIPS

The most obvious advantage of an athletic scholarship is that it pays for college. This is not a minor consideration given the enormous cost of higher education. In addition, there are also personal advantages that come with an athletic scholarship.

Mike Terrizzi, former Purdue punter and quarterback (who still holds the record for the longest punt at Notre Dame's stadium), looks back on his football scholarship as more than a means of paying the bill. "The scholarship gave me a real sense of accomplishment," he says. "I felt like I was being paid back for a lot of hard work. I also think my scholarship gave a name to my high school program. It helped bring more college scouts sniffing around and it helped younger players get into better colleges. I can't explain how good it felt to be appreciated for doing what I loved to do, and to help athletes who came after me."

Terrizzi's feelings are shared by many former college athletes. When asked about the advantages of an athletic scholarship they all mention factors such as personal pride, prestige, achievement, fulfillment and success. But Terrizzi and most others also now look back and realize that the athletic scholarship is not offered only in admiration of talent; it's offered as a business deal.

Full athletic scholarships—the ones that pay all the educational expenses of college—are offered almost exclusively by only the larger, Division I-type schools. These schools don't "give"the money away. They put it down as a calculated gamble. The coaches bet that the money they invest in an athlete's talents will pay off in the creation of a championship team. Championship teams automatically bring money into the college. They attract media coverage and support, which quickly turns into increased alumni donations, soaring ticket sales, better collegiate image and increased enrollment.

Georgia Tech is a good example of how an athletic team can bring money into the college. In 1991 the football team finished number one in the coach's poll after compiling the only undefeated record (11–0–1) in major-college football. The following season Tech sold out all 24,000 season tickets for the first time in almost 20 years and applications for enrollment were up about 15 percent at a time when enrollment at most universities was down. The money Tech had paid in scholarships for these team members obviously was well worth the gamble.

Athletic scholarships may pay the bill, boost athletes' egos and build strong teams, but they come with strings attached. They are given in the expectation that the athletes will continue to meet the athletic standards of the team. To do this consistently, team members give up some personal freedoms: the freedom to quit the team and still claim a free education, the freedom to take it easy once in a while, sometimes the freedom to weigh what they'd like and to eat what they'd like. Even the freedom to disagree with a coach or a policy is severely limited. Athletic scholarships aren't given for free; scholarship athletes owe the school and they owe the coach. Sometimes this debt is burdensome.

Mary Conklin found this out the hard way. Mary was a serious student who wanted a good education and found that she could afford the selective college of her choice if she played basketball. When the coaches assured Mary that academics would always come before basketball, she gladly enrolled and signed onto the team. But while traveling to an away game in the middle of her first season, Mary came face to face with the hidden cost of her scholarship. Conklin took a seat in the back of the bus so she could use the travel time to study. Without warning the assistant coach stormed down the aisle, ripped the book from Mary's hands and after tossing it out the window yelled at Mary for not keeping her mind on the upcoming game. Mary played the game but then packed her bags the next morning and headed home. She needed time to decide if she could continue to take money for an education that she felt pressured to ignore. Although I would guess she may have had other problems with the team and school, after this incident Mary Conklin withdrew from the college and enrolled in a school she could afford. She decided the cost of her scholarship was too high.

You should also remember that athletic scholarships are not a guaranteed passport through college. They are given for one year only and must be renewed by a financial aid authority of the athletic department at the end of each year. Coaches may assure athletes that they will recommend scholarship renewal each year, but they also have the obligation to inform every athlete that the renewal is not automatic.

When choosing the one school you'll attend, the conditions under which a scholarship can be denied renewal should be one of your major considerations—the reasons vary from school to school and even from player to player. Although most schools can't bump a player for poor athletic performance, they can refuse renewal for many other reasons. You can lose an athletic scholarship if you don't continually meet the academic requirements of the college and the athletic association. You can lose it if the coach feels you've developed a bad attitude, or if you miss practices, or if you engage in unacceptable behavior or become a discipline problem. You can also lose your scholarship if you become ineligible for competition through illness or injury—this is probably the area of greatest concern for scholarship athletes.

If you're offered an athletic scholarship make sure you understand the conditions under which you can lose it. It's tempting to jump at the full scholarship and turn down a partial one, but consider all factors first. If you can lose your full scholarship when you sprain your ankle walking to class, but can keep your partial one no matter how or where you're injured, the partial one may be the better choice. If you'd have to drop out of school if you lose your full scholarship but could afford to stay at the school that takes away a partial one, again the partial one might be better.

In Chapter Three I suggested that you choose schools that fit all your needs and that you can afford to attend even if you weren't given an athletic scholarship. Here, I'll repeat that advice. An athletic scholarship is a wonderful opportunity only when it's offered by a college that fits your athletic and academic abilities and one that you would enjoy and could afford through other sources of financial aid even if you're cut from the team. As long as you understand the responsibilities and risks that go along with athletic scholarships, then you can use them to get where you want to go.

THE FACTS ABOUT ATHLETIC SCHOLARSHIPS

All schools that offer athletic scholarships follow one very inflexible rule: A student-athlete can receive no more financial aid than the actual cost of (1) tuition, (2) mandatory fees, (3) required books and supplies and (4) room and board. An athletic scholarship that exceeds this amount is in violation of all college, university and athletic association rules. If a coach offers you $1,000 for "books" you might at first think, "What a great deal." But remember the warning from Chapter Five: Don't get involved with any coach who offers you money worth more than the educational expenses of the college. That kind of financial aid is an illegal recruiting offer that can kill your athletic eligibility.

Beyond this one common rule, other aspects of athletic scholarships vary from school to school. Some general guidelines can be offered, however, by looking at the way the various associations and divisions of intercollegiate athletics offer scholarships.

NCAA ATHLETIC SCHOLARSHIPS

The NCAA has very exact rules governing the offering of financial aid to student-athletes. The list of these rules covers 20 pages in the NCAA Manual. Rather than report them all here, I recommend that you get a copy of the manual from your high school coach or ask the college coach who's recruiting you to send you a copy of Bylaw

Article 15 for your own use. The following sections will give you an idea of how the money in NCAA schools is awarded to athletes.

Ivy League Schools and Division III Sports

All Ivy League schools (Brown, Columbia, Cornell, Darmouth, Harvard, University of Pennsylvania, Princeton and Yale) and Division III sports do NOT give any athletic scholarships. But if you want to go to one of these schools, don't cross them off your list right away just because you need financial aid. They do have other ways of helping athletes pay the bill; all of the schools give need-based financial aid. The aid is offered as blind-need, which means the amount is calculated the same for every student regardless of special talents such as athletic ability. But because they don't offer athletic scholarships, the size of these financial aid packages can be larger for financially needy students than those offered at other schools. Jeffrey Orleans, Executive Director of the Council of Ivy Group Presidents, explains that this can happen because the NCAA limits athletic scholarships to the cost of tuition, room and board, fees and books only. Therefore the athletic grant may cover less than the financial aid packages offered at nonscholarship schools who can pay the full cost of attending college, which includes personal expenses such as laundry money, clothing and travel costs. So sometimes a financial aid package can offer more than an athletic scholarship.

Although the coaches often help their recruited athletes fill out the forms to qualify for these need-based financial aid packages, the awards are not tied in any way to athletic performance. Once you are given financial aid from a Division III or Ivy school, the aid stays in effect even if you quit the team or become permanently disabled.

Division I and II Scholarships

NCAA Division I and II schools offer the majority of all athletic scholarships in the United States. Division I schools are known to give most of the full scholarships awarded each year while Division IIs often choose to give partial ones, which cover some but not all educational expenses. At both level schools, the number of scholar-

DIVISION I MEN'S SPORTS		DIVISION II MEN'S SPORTS	
baseball	11.7	baseball	10
basketball	13.0	basketball	12
cross country/track	12.6	cross country/track	16
fencing	4.5	fencing	5
football I-A	88.0	football	40
football I-AA	65.0		
golf	4.5	golf	4
gymnastics	6.3	gymnastics	6
ice hockey	18.0	ice hockey	15
lacrosse	12.6	lacrosse	12
rifle	3.6	rifle	4
skiing	6.3	skiing	7
soccer	9.9	soccer	10
swimming	9.9	swimming	9
tennis	4.5	tennis	5
volleyball	4.5	volleyball	5
water polo	4.5	water polo	5
wrestling	9.9	wrestling	10

ships and their dollar amounts are determined by the NCAA restrictions on the number of scholarships allowed in effect at one time.

Division I schools can maintain superior teams because they have the scholarship advantage. A I-A football team during the 1993–94 season, for example, can have 88 full scholarships in effect at any one time, but Division II football teams are allowed only 40. When a coach tells a young high school athlete who is recruited late in the senior year, "I'd love to give you a scholarship, but I can't because there's no money left," the player may think, "If he really wanted me, he'd come up with the money." Well, it's not usually a matter

DIVISION I WOMEN'S SPORTS		DIVISION II WOMEN'S SPORTS	
basketball	13.0	basketball	12
cross country/track	14.4	cross country/track	14
fencing	4.5	fencing	5
field hockey	9.9	field hockey	7
golf	5.4	golf	6
gymnastics	10.0	gymnastics	6
lacrosse	9.9	lacrosse	11
skiing	6.3	skiing	7
soccer	9.9	soccer	11
softball	9.9	softball	8
swimming	12.6	swimming	9
tennis	8.0	tennis	6
volleyball	12.0	volleyball	8

of want; it's a matter of fact. The NCAA has set the limits (see boxes above and page 114) on scholarship awards that can be in effect at any one time during the 1993–94 academic year.

These are the maximum awards allowed under the NCAA rules governing financial aid. Don't be discouraged, however, if you're looking for a golf scholarship and see that Division I schools are allowed only four and a half scholarships spread among all members of the college team. Many schools choose to break up the total number into many smaller, partial scholarships.

Your ability to obtain any financial aid based on your athletic skills at Division I or Division II schools depends of course on your ability to meet the NCAA academic eligibility requirements of Bylaw 14.3 listed in Chapter Five. Depending on your high school academic standing, you will be labeled a qualifier, a partial qualifier or a nonqualifier. A qualifier is a student who meets all the requirements and is therefore eligible without restrictions to participate in intercollegiate athletics and receive financial aid based on athletic ability. If you are a partial-qualifer or a nonqualifier, your scholarship opportunities are restricted.

A *Division I partial qualifier* is one who has not met all of the academic requirements listed in Chapter Five but who has graduated from high school with an overall grade-point average of 2.000. This athlete may not receive an athletic scholarship but may receive need-based aid from the school's financial aid department.

A *Division I nonqualifier* is one who has not met all the academic eligibility requirements or has not graduated from high school with an overall grade-point average of 2.000. This student may not receive financial aid of any kind. No institutional, need-based, athletic or merit aid is allowed.

A *Division II partial qualifer* is one who has not met all the eligibility requirements but who has graduated from high school and has fulfilled either the required core-curriculum or standardized test-score requirement. This student may receive both institutional need-based financial aid and athletic-related financial aid.

A *Division II nonqualifier* is one who has not met all of the eligibility requirements or has not graduated from high school with an overall grade-point average of 2.000. This student may receive institutional financial aid that is not related to athletic ability.

In addition to the athletic scholarships offered at NCAA schools, student-athletes may also receive additional financing from the government and miscellaneous sources explained later in this chapter. This is acceptable as long as the aid is not given based on athletic ability and does not exceed the cost of the education. Be sure to talk with the college financial aid officer to find out how you can combine financial aid sources to cover the full cost of your education.

Need-based Athletic Scholarships

Some schools offer athletic scholarships based on financial need rather than athletic ability. This sounds like Division III and Ivy grants, but it's different. Let's say an Ivy League school offers a soccer player $10,000 in financial aid; the financial aid officer may break the aid into a $3,000 work study, a $3,000 loan and a $4,000 grant.

While the financial aid officer at colleges where athletic scholarships are need-based may determine that this same student is eligible for the same $10,000 in aid, the *coach* decides how to break it up. The coach may decide to give this athlete a $4,000 loan and a $6,000 grant, or even a full $10,000 grant. Although coaches can't offer an amount that exceeds the determined financial need, this system obviously gives coaches a great deal of input in how financially needy athletes are given athletic scholarships. Quite a number of schools give need-based athletic scholarships. They include colleges like Lehigh, Lafayette, Bucknell, Colgate and Holy Cross.

Nonscholarship Schools

In 1991, some Division II schools found it financially draining to offer football scholarships valuable enough to attract top athletes and stay competitive in their leagues. Rather than eliminate their football programs or change them to club teams, the East Coast Athletic Conference came up with a third option. They formed an intercollegiate, nonscholarship football conference, which begins play in 1993. The league includes 11 schools with Division I sports: St. Peter's, Brooklyn College, Canisius, Central Connecticut State, Duquesne, Iona, Marist, St. Francis (Pennsylvania), St. John's, Siena and Wagner; and nine Division II schools: Assumption, Bentley, Gannon, Massachusetts-Lowell, Mercyhurst, Pace, C.W. Post, Sacred Heart and Stonehill.

As costs rise and budgets shrink, more schools may follow this path. So don't assume all NCAA Division I and II schools offer athletic scholarships. Be sure to ask each recruiting coach if the college gives athletic scholarships in your sport. If the answer is yes then ask if the college has any future plans of eliminating the sport, changing it to a club or intramural sport or joining a nonscholarship conference.

NAIA ATHLETIC SCHOLARSHIPS

The National Association of Intercollegiate Athletics is a group of schools generally smaller in size than NCAA schools. This is why they don't offer as attractive or as lucrative athletic scholarships as

NCAA Division I sports. But most NAIA schools do give athletic scholarships so they shouldn't be overlooked in your search for good schools that offer financial aid to athletes.

In the past, the number of athletic scholarships allowed in each NAIA sport was not regulated. However, beginning in the 1993–94 academic year the NAIA has restricted the number of scholarships allowed in effect at any one time in the following sports:

Baseball	12	Swimming & Diving	8
Basketball (Division I)	12	Tennis	4
Cross Country (only)	3	Track & Field (only)	7
Football (Division I)	33	Track & Field &	
Golf	4	Cross Country	10
Soccer	12	Volleyball	12
Softball	12	Wrestling	6

(As of Winter 1993, limits for Division II basketball and football had yet to be determined by the NAIA Council of Presidents.)

Like NCAA schools, the NAIA schools can give these scholarships in full or partial amounts.

ADMISSION "SCHOLARSHIPS"

For some athletes the guarantee of admission to the college of their choice is as good as gold. If you want your athletic abilities to open the doors to colleges, consider admission your "scholarship" and be just as careful about what coaches offer in admission advantages as you would be in financial matters.

It doesn't mean anything if a coach says, "I'll recommend you for admission." Get a guarantee. Ask, "Will I be on your preferred list?" Some schools like the College of William and Mary have admission slots that coaches can use for their recruits; if the coach says, "I'll give you one of my admission slots," you'll get in. Some California state universities use the term "tagging"; if your application is tagged by a coach, you'll get in. Other schools like Swarthmore College use a ranking numerical system from one to

ATHLETIC SCHOLARSHIP INFORMATION

School _____

Date _____

1. Are you able to offer me an athletic scholarship? _____
   (If the answer is "No" ask about other sources of financial aid as explained below. If the answer is "Yes" continue with these questions.)
2. What exactly does a full scholarship cover?_____
   _____
   b. What is its dollar amount? _____
3. How much of my educational cost will be covered by a partial scholarship in my sport? _____
   b. What is its dollar amount? _____
4. Does the scholarship include medical coverage in season? _____
   b. off season? _____
5. What criteria must I meet to have my scholarship renewed?
   _____
6. Will my scholarship be withdrawn if I become injured or ill?
   _____
7. If I don't get a scholarship in my freshman year what are the chances that I might be awarded one in my sophomore year?
   _____
   _____
8. Do you have a summer job-placement service for athletes?
   _____
9. When will I know if I will receive an athletic scholarship to your school? _____

five; if the coach ranks you a 5, you'll get in. Before you consider a promise of admission to be money in the bank, make sure you're on that preferred list.

QUESTIONS TO ASK ABOUT ATHLETIC SCHOLARSHIPS

If you do want to get an athletic scholarship, don't sit around waiting for it to knock on your door. Tell the recruiting coaches that you need financial aid and be prepared to get all the details that will help you make your final decision. Don't accept a coach's promise of, "We'll work out something." Ask the specific questions listed on page 119 and write in the answers so you can compare schools. Be sure each coach gives you exact answers before you commit to any one.

If the answers to these questions still leave you without enough money to finance your education, don't give up. Look to other sources of financial aid that may fill the gap.

OTHER SOURCES OF FINANCIAL AID

The majority of collegiate athletes don't have athletic scholarships. Many do, however, receive financial aid from the institution, the government or from other outside sources. These financial aid packages generally contain three kinds of aid:

Grants or scholarships: These are sources of aid that are given without strings attached; you do not have to pay them back.

Loans: This money must be repaid after graduation or leaving school. Student loans have lower interest rates than commercial loans.

Work: On- or off-campus employment can be arranged by the college to help students meet their financial obligations.

All three types of aid can be obtained from the following sources:

Institutional Aid

The first place you should look for additional financial aid is at the college itself. Most college applications include a financial aid form that you should read over carefully with your parents; you'll need their input to fill in the financial information section. Then fill it out and send it in.

You'll also be instructed to complete and submit another detailed financial form. Most colleges request either the Financial Aid Form (FAF) or the Family Financial Statement (FFS), which are available from your guidance counselor. When completed, send it as directed to either the College Scholarship Service or the American College Testing Program; these organizations analyze your family's financial needs and send the results to the colleges of your choice. Based on these reports, the colleges will consider what you can afford to pay for your education against the total cost of attending their schools. The remainder is what they will try to give you in a financial aid package.

Federal and State Aid

The government offers undergraduate college students a variety of federal and state financial aid programs to help pay the cost of a college education.

The federal government offers Pell Grants and Supplemental Educational Opportunity Grants (SEOG), which are rewarded based on financial need, range in value from $100 to $4,000 a year and are renewable each year. You must apply for SEOG through the financial aid office at each college. Applications for Pell Grants are available from your guidance department or the college financial aid office, or by writing to the Federal Student Aid Information Center, P.O. Box 84, Washington, D.C. 20044.

Pell Grant money is a factor you should carefully investigate before you choose your college. NCAA regulations allow Division I athletes to add Pell Grant money up to $1,700 onto their athletic scholarship even if this addition amounts to more than the cost of tuition, room and board, fees and books; Division II athletes are able to add on up to $900 of Pell Grant money. This gives an athlete some personal spending money. Although technically allowable, some schools have institutional rules that will not allow a student to add the money onto an athletic scholarship and so they deduct the government grant from their scholarship offer. If you are applying for a Pell Grant ask the recruiting coaches if you will be allowed to keep the money if it is awarded to you.

Other government backed financial aid programs include the following:

- Perkins Loans are low-interest loans made to students through the college's financial aid office. Repayment and interest begin nine months after you graduate, leave school or drop below half-time enrollment.

- Stafford Loans allow eligible students to borrow from any participating lender, and the state or a private nonprofit agency will guarantee the loan. The federal government pays the interest on the loan while you're in school. Repayment and interest payments begin six months after you graduate, leave school or drop below half-time enrollment.
- PLUS loans allow a parent or independent undergraduate student to borrow from a bank or other lender with a state or other private nonprofit agency guaranteeing the loan. The federal government does not pay the interest on the loan while the student is in school. Repayment and interest payments begin 60 days after the loan is given.
- College work-study programs provide jobs for students who need financial aid. Under this program the employer pays a small part of the student's wages and the government pays the rest. You can apply for work-study jobs through the college financial aid office.

In addition to these national programs each state has its own financial aid system to offer grants, loans and competitive scholarships. Ask your guidance counselor about the programs available to you or write to the state scholarship agency in your state capitol.

Miscellaneous Sources

In addition to college- and government-funded financial aid, you may be eligible for scholarship money offered by other sources. In any guidance department, library or bookstore you'll find published guides that list hundreds of scholarship opportunities; surely there's one for you. There is one, for example, from AMVETS that gives aid to the dependent children of American war veterans; another from the Burger King Crew Member Scholarship Program that awards scholarships to Burger King employees; the Graphic Arts Technical Foundation Program offers scholarships to students studying graphic arts; and the National Ambucs Scholarship Program provides financial assistance to students enrolled in occupational or physical therapy programs. The list goes on and on so it takes time to read through the hundreds of opportunities looking for ones that fit you and your goals—but they're there if you look.

If you don't have time to search for extra money, you can hire a scholarship service to do the job for you. For a fee ranging from $40 to $100 these services use computers to find the scholarships that are offered to students of your sex, ethnic origin, financial background, academic standing and with your special talents, interests and future goals. You still have to do the work of contacting the scholarship sponsors and filling out their applications but the service saves you the bother of finding the sources. If you want more information about scholarship services ask your guidance counselor for the phone number of one in your area. But be careful. Some services are rip-offs that pass along outdated or useless information. A call to your local Better Business Bureau before sending off your check might save you some time and money.

Don't overlook your own community when looking for financial aid. Most local organizations such as the Elks, Rotary Club, Lions Club and women's clubs offer scholarships. The applications are usually distributed through the high school guidance department for interested students. Be sure to let your counselor know you're interested.

A word of caution, however, before I send you off looking for miscellaneous scholarships. Consider this story of a local track star: Using the results of her FAF forms, the financial aid office at a Division III school determined that the girl's family could contribute $3,000 toward her education; the school then offered her another $3,000 in financial aid to cover the remainder of the total $6,000 bill.

To help her family pay their $3,000 share, the athlete spent a great deal of time and effort applying for scholarship money from outside sources. She filled in about 30 applications, wrote essays, gathered the recommendations, even went on interviews and took examinations. In the end, she thought her efforts paid off when she pulled together a total of $5,000 from several different sources giving her $2,000 over her college costs for living expenses.

However, the way the financial aid system is organized, the athlete could not add that money on top of her financial aid package. She now had enough money to pay her own educational expenses and so her efforts eliminated the college's obligation to offer any financial aid. The college took away her $3,000 and her family was left $1,000 short. This isn't cruel or unreasonable; it's just the way the system works. So if you expect to receive financial aid from government or institutional sources, ask a financial aid officer how the college calculates outside scholarships into their financial award decisions.

COMPARE AND SAVE

Let's imagine that you've been accepted for admission at three schools all equal in academic and athletic opportunities. College A has offered you a $9,000 athletic scholarship; College B has offered a financial package that includes a student loan and a work-study program worth $6,000. And College C can give you no financial aid at all. Which school would you choose?

COLLEGE A   **TOTAL COST: $17,000**

Your contribution
(as determined by your FAF) $ 3,000
athletic scholarship   9,000
                                                       $12,000

Subtract this $12,000 from the total cost of $17.000 and the *cost left unpaid is $5,000.*

COLLEGE B   **TOTAL COST: $10,000**

Your contribution $ 3,000
financial aid   6,000
                                                       $ 9,000

Subtract this $9,000 from the total cost of $10,000 and the *cost left unpaid is $1,000.*

COLLEGE C   **TOTAL COST: $ 9,000**

Your contribution $ 3,000
financial aid   0
                                                       $ 3,000

Subtract this $3,000 from the total cost of $9,000 and the *cost left unpaid is $6,000.*

College A sounds best to me. But if we take time to really compare the three offerings, we'll get a better view of the whole financial picture.

Now, College B looks like the best buy leaving only $1,000 unpaid. But there's more information to consider. College B is the furthest away from home, which could add high travel and phone expenses. And College C has a summer job-placement service for athletes that can put you in a job related to your academic field of interest and pay you up to $5,000 each summer. Now, College C, which at first seemed like the worst choice, will cost the same as College B but without the added travel expenses and will give job experience that may be useful after graduation but will not interfere with classes or athletics during the college term.

Although no three colleges can really be exactly the same because factors such as campus appearance, course offerings and even the coach's personality will play roles in your final decision, financially

---

CHECKLIST TO FINANCIAL AID

Use this checklist to help you get all the facts about the financial aid situation at each college you apply to. Make copies of this worksheet and put it in the folders you've organized in earlier chapters for each college. Then put a check next to each step as you complete it.

1. Choose colleges based on your academic and athletic abilities and goals. Include at least two back-up schools that you can afford and where you know you will be admitted. _____
2. Apply to the colleges and return the financial aid forms included in the application packets. _____
3. Request financial aid from coaches at each college who have shown recruiting interest. _____
4. Submit FAF or FFS applications well before the deadline. _____
5. Apply for federal and state financial aid through your high school guidance department or the college's financial aid office. _____
6. Look for local and specialized scholarship sources; obtain, complete and return the applications. _____
7. Wait until all financial aid offers are in; weigh the pros and cons of each before making any financial decisions. _____

speaking, College C, which offered no financial aid and which at first seemed out of the picture, is probably the best choice.

The point is: Don't be blinded by large numbers; look at all the pieces and compare all factors before you discard any offers.

This information will help you find the money to finance your education. But remember, the availability of athletic scholarships and financial aid should not be the primary reason for choosing one school over another. There are many academic factors to consider and, as you'll find in the following chapter, there are also many athletic considerations besides money that should be discussed with the college coaches before you make your final decision.

CHAPTER 9

MAKING THE FINAL DECISION

The twin sisters grabbed sports-page headlines early in their basketball career. Outstanding talent and national exposure made Zoya and Jeaneen highly recruited, blue-chip athletes; they had college offers from large universities and small country colleges, from city commuter schools and ocean-front resort schools. By the end of their sophomore year the girls' father and high school coach knew they needed an organized system to narrow down their college prospects.

They designed a checklist similar to the worksheet in Chapter Three. It helped the girls decide what kind of education they wanted, what kind of environment they wanted to live in and what kind of basketball program they wanted to play for.

Still, by their junior-year season, the girls had an overload of offers. Then Zoya, the more heavily recruited sister, added a factor that helped narrow the list. She decided that she would not attend any college or university that did not give her sister an athletic scholarship also. In addition to academic, social and athletic needs, Zoya decided that she needed to be with her sister. This package-deal criteria reduced the number of scholarship offers and helped the girls make their final decision.

Like Zoya and Jeaneen, as a student-athlete in your senior year, you'll need to find criteria that will put one school above all others. For some athletes that one thing will be a gut feeling; for others it will be something very specific.

By mid-May of your senior year, you should have all the information you need to make your final decision. (Early decision applicants need to gather this information by mid-September of their senior year.) If you have the talent and have played the recruiting game wisely and thoroughly, by this time you will have received letters of college acceptance along with the coaches' offers of a spot on the team, and you'll have your final financial aid information. At that point it will be time to choose one college above all others.

SELECTION CRITERIA

Before you choose that one college, let's regroup a minute and make sure that all the schools on your final list meet the five selection-criteria factors outlined in Chapter Three:

1. Academic Suitability
   - Regardless of the athletic eligibility rules and the fact that you've been accepted, do you meet the colleges' academic requirements?
   - Do the colleges all offer a major in your field of interest?
   - Would you want to attend this college or university if you weren't participating in the athletic program?
2. Cost
   - Will you be able to afford each college through other sources of financial aid if you decide not to participate in athletics or if you become injured and ineligible for an athletic scholarship?
   - Have you carefully compared all financial aid offers?
3. Location
   - Have you visited each campus?
   - Could you live comfortably at each school?

- Have you considered the cost and inconvenience of traveling to and from distant schools?

4. Size
    - Have you spent enough time on campus to get a good feeling for how its size fits your academic and social needs?

5. Athletic Program
    - Do the schools compete on a level that matches your ability?
    - Do the athletic programs match the goals you set in Chapter One?

THE ATHLETIC PROGRAM

If you're in a position to choose among several colleges that meet your academic, social, and financial needs, then the finer details of the athletic program may become your deciding factor.

To help make the final decision, first examine each team as you would a sorority or fraternity. Do you like the people? When you spent time with team members during your campus visit, did they appear friendly or conceited? Were they helpful or showy? Would you feel comfortable spending most of your time with them?

Think also about the coaches. Can you talk to the coach about important and personal things? Has the coach made a habit of promising the world and delivering very little? Does the coach talk through assistant coaches or does he or she give you some individual attention?

The answers to these questions are important. As a collegiate athlete you'll be working and socializing with these people for four years—your stay at college will be happier if you like them.

When you're sure you "fit" the athletic program, make copies of Worksheet 4 on page 130 and label each with the names of your final-choice colleges. Then have a long talk with the coaches from each school and ask them the following questions. Don't worry that you'll sound too picky; most coaches will be impressed that you care enough about your athletic career to ask for the details.

An honest evaluation of the answers to these questions will help you be realistic about what you can offer a team and it will make you

---

WORKSHEET #4

Athletic Program

SCHOOL _____

1. When and for how long does the team practice? (6:00 A.M. practices are not uncommon!) _____

2. Are the practice facilities adequate and freely available? _____

3. What is the length of the season schedule? _____
   - How many away competitions are there? _____
   - How many league competitions are there? _____
   - How many non-league competitions are there? _____
   - How many post-season competitions are there? _____

4. What is the competitive strength of the team:
   - Does it have a winning tradition? _____
   - Is it in a rebuilding stage? _____

5. How much playing time will I get? _____
   - How many seniors are graduating? _____
   - How many new recruits are scheduled for my position? _____
   - What does the depth chart in my position look like?

   _____

---

be honest with yourself about what you want out of an athletic program.

Frank McLaughlin knows from experience that it's extremely important for athletes to be realistic about where they fit. Before becoming the Director of Athletics at Fordham University, McLaughlin spent six years as the assistant basketball coach at Notre Dame and eight years as the head coach at Harvard. "There's nothing worse," he says, "than going to play on a college team and finding yourself unhappy. It affects everything—even your academics and your social life. Take a basketball player, for example. If he goes to Indiana and finds out he's the 14th guy on the team, the next thing you know he's struggling in school; he's homesick and he's unhappy. But if he had gone to a level below Indiana he might be a star or at least a starter and he'd do better academically and personally." Take it from people who know—the athletes who ask a lot of questions, match the answers to their own expectations and needs and choose the college that's the most realistic fit are the happiest during their college years.

AN UNHAPPY FIT

It was an unrealistic match in 1991 that made news headlines at Ohio State. Robert Smith, who had the year before shattered the Buckeyes' 18-year freshman football rushing record with 1,126 yards, began his sophomore year planning to transfer to a Division III university within commuting distance from his home. The reason: the 40 hours a week that football required didn't leave Smith enough time to concentrate on his pre-med studies. The news accounts pointed to a scandal when Smith accused the coaches of pressuring him to miss class to attend football practice and of yelling, "You're here to play football."

According to *Sports Illustrated*, Smith had clearly defined reasons for being in college and football was not on the top of that list. The article stated, "Before visiting Columbus as a recruit, Smith informed the Buckeye staff that he was not interested in touring the weight room, sampling the training-table fare or ogling Griffin's two Heismans. Smith wanted to see the medical school, talk to ordinary students and stroll through the library."

Because Smith planned to play football at Ohio, he should not have ignored the athletic components of his future college life. Even though his primary interest put academics over athletics, it's too bad Smith didn't think to ask more questions of the coaches and team members. He should have talked to athletes about how much time they spent on the practice field and about how the coaches treated players and regarded academics. He should have talked with pre-med faculty members who surely could have warned him that the football schedule would make it extremely difficult to fulfill his course requirements. And given Ohio's reputation as a tough football school and the known pressure on the coaches to build a winning team, Smith was probably naive to think that his football scholarship wouldn't oblige him to put in the weekly 40 hours of practice time.

Don't be naive. Ask lots of questions and make sure the answers match your goals before you enroll.

THE FINAL CHOICE

In September of his senior year, Roy Hopkins narrowed down his college list to four schools: Stoney Hill University, Beacon University, Rollinger University and State College (the actual colleges have been given pseudonyms). Roy's final decision wasn't an easy one because although the baseball coaches at each of these schools assured Roy they had a place on their team for him, each school had its advantages and disadvantages.

All four colleges fit most of Roy's selection criteria listed on his Worksheet from Chapter Three. All cost less than $12,000. All are in the east. All are in rural or suburban areas. All offer a major in communications.

Stoney Hill and Beacon also matched Roy's academic ability with required miminum combined average SAT scores of 903 and 920— close enough to Roy's 850 to assure a good academic fit. Both also fielded Division II baseball teams (Roy's evaluated level) and offered athletic scholarships.

The State College didn't offer Roy a scholarship because it's a Division III school. But it's a local college that Roy could commute to so the cost would be an affordable $2,765. State College was Roy's fall-back school. He knew he could afford it, would do well there academically and could play baseball on a team with a strong winning tradition in a very competitive league. But because it's a Division III commuter school, Roy didn't really want to go there.

Rollinger University was Roy's reach school. It was above his academic level with average combined SATs of 1115. It's Division I baseball team was also above his evaluated athletic level. But Roy had been offered admission and a spot on the team so he wanted to keep it on his final selection list.

The financial picture at each school gave Roy more factors to consider before making his final decision.

- Stoney Hill offered Roy a one-year, renewable partial athletic scholarship that would pay $4,234 of the total $8,318. So Roy needed $4,084 to enroll.
- Beacon University offered Roy a one-year, renewable financial aid package that included a $1,500 grant and a $2,000 loan. Roy would have to pay $4,300 of the total $7,800 bill.
- State College did not offer Roy any financial aid and so he would have to pay the full $2,765.
- Rollinger University's athletic department didn't offer Roy an athletic scholarship. The financial aid office put together a package that gave Roy a total of $4,554, leaving him to pay a $6,286 balance.

Rollinger's financial picture put the university further out of Roy's reach. Not only was the school above his athletic and academic level; it also would be the most expensive. Still Roy wanted to keep it in the running.

Roy eliminated State College from his list because, although it cost less than the others, his family could afford to send him to either Stoney Hill or Beacon even if he lost the scholarship. Beacon would initially cost about the same as Stoney Hill, but part of the financial aid was a loan that Roy would have to pay back. So all things considered, Stoney Hill looked like the best choice.

The last factor to consider came down to the athletic programs. Roy called the coaches at Stoney Hill, Beacon, and Rollinger and asked the questions on Worksheet 4. When the answers were compared, Roy was finally ready to eliminate Rollinger. The coach told Roy that he didn't expect to start him for at least two years. At both Stoney Hill and Beacon Roy was assured a place in the pitching rotation and Roy discovered that both schools played in highly respected and competitive leagues. Although Roy's ego liked the idea of being on a Division I team, he didn't want to sit the bench for two years and so he crossed Rollinger off the list.

Now faced with choosing between Stoney Hill and Beacon, Roy looked back to his campus experience as the deciding factor. The more he thought about it and compared his visitation notes, Roy liked Stoney Hill. He liked the students, the team members, the coach, the professors and the campus. Although he couldn't point to anything specific about Beacon that he didn't like, he chose Stoney Hill because it felt right.

CONFIRM YOUR DECISION

Once Roy made his final decision, there were still a few steps to complete before he finished the admissions process. First Roy contacted Stoney Hill's baseball coach to accept the athletic scholarship. He also notified the admissions office of his intent to enroll and sent the required deposit money. Then as a gesture of common courtesy, Roy contacted all the other colleges and coaches and told them of his plans to attend Stoney Hill.

Roy thought that once he told the college coaches he was going to Stoney Hill, the recruiting process would end, but it didn't. He continued to hear from coaches and players and alumni who tried to make him change his mind. This persistent recruiting, which tries to lure athletes away from their chosen schools and keeps high school students from concentrating on their school work and their sports, used to continue throughout the year, into the summer, and even follow the athletes into their chosen college. But today over 450 Division I and II institutions voluntarily participate in the National Letter of Intent Program, which has put an end to incessant recruiting.

THE NATIONAL LETTER OF INTENT PROGRAM

The National Letter of Intent (NLI) is an official document administered by the Collegiate Commissioners Association, which, when signed by the prospective athlete, his or her parents and the Athletic Director of the institution, certifies that the student will enroll in a certain school. All cooperating conferences and institutions agree to respect this decision and not attempt to recruit the athlete further.

Once Roy signed his letter in April, the recruiting process stopped and he was free to play his senior year baseball season without giving another thought to recruiters and performance evaluations.

To be eligible to sign an offered National Letter of Intent, certain requirements must be met. The student-athlete must satisfy the institution's and the NCAA's requirements for college admission and athletic participation. If the athlete is being offered a scholarship or other form of financial aid, he or she must, before signing, receive in writing an award or recommendation for this aid from the institution. (If the recommended financial aid is not approved within the institution's normal time period for awarding aid, the NLI becomes invalid.)

The NLI is intended to benefit recruited student-athletes, but it also protects the institution. Athletes who sign an NLI are bound to that college; if they change their mind the penalty for breaking the agreement can destroy an athletic career. If an athlete who signs an NLI does not attend the named institution and decides instead to enroll in another institution participating in the NLI program, that athlete may not represent the enrolled college in any intercollegiate competition in any sport until completing two full academic years at that institution.

You will not sign an NLI as soon as you make your decision to attend a Division I or II school. The signing periods are strictly prescribed by the Collegiate Commissioners Association. Currently, the signing periods follow this schedule:

- Men's and women's basketball prospects sign on a given date (the exact day varies from year to year) starting in mid-April and continuing through mid-May.
- Football players sign from a given date in the first week of February until April 1.
- Soccer, water polo, field hockey and women's volleyball sign on a given date in the first week of February through August 1.
- All other sports sign from a given date in mid-April until August 1.

Some sports allow an early signing date, which stops the recruiting process in the fall and allows an athlete to concentrate on the senior year in high school rather than on recruiting. The sports and dates currently available for early signing are:

- Men's and women's basketball prospects can sign during one given week in mid-November.
- All other sports not specifically named above can also sign during one given week in mid-November.

Early signing is most helpful to highly recruited athletes who have their pick of quality schools and are absolutely sure where they want to go early in their senior year. Early signing keeps recruiters off their backs so they can enjoy their senior year. But because it does take them out of the running, these athletes should either apply for early decision to their chosen school so they can get back into the recruiting arena if they're denied admission, or they should feel fully qualified to meet the admission requirements. If after signing an NLI a student is not admitted to the school the NLI becomes invalid.

Early signing is not always advantageous. Many student-athletes are not sure at the beginning of their senior year exactly where they want to go and an early signing would commit them to something they may not want a full year later. Also, a good senior-year sport season can improve an athlete's collegiate prospects and recruitability. Athletes who sign early with a Division II school, for example, and then become outstanding players in their last season have given up their right to be recruited by Division I coaches.

Whether you plan to sign early or on the regular schedule, be absolutely sure before you put your name on the line. This document is honored by all member schools and strictly binds you to your agreement.

Non-participating Schools

Some colleges do not participate in the National Letter of Intent Program—most notably all Division III schools, Ivy League schools, military service academies and NAIA schools. If you choose to go to one of these colleges, you will sign an agreement with the athletic director but it isn't binding. If after signing with a Division III or NAIA school, for example, you are offered admission to a Division

I or II school, you can enroll in the school without forfeiting any intercollegiate athletic eligibility. In the same way, if you sign an NLI but then change your mind and decide you'd rather attend an Ivy League school, you can enroll in an Ivy school and participate in the athletic program without penalty.

The National Letter of Intent Program is something prospective college athletes should fully understand. Ask your high school and college coach to go over every detail of the agreement before you sign it. Once it's signed it gives you freedom to enjoy your senior year, but it also commits you to one institution. So be sure before you sign.

GOOD LUCK

Whew! Finally, by the end of April in the senior year the recruiting and admission process is completed for most student-athletes. If you've followed the process explained in this book, you will have made a choice based on objective criteria, careful consideration of your goals and needs and a final dose of personal feelings. Your chances of staying at college and graduating are greatly increased when you go knowing why you're going and what's there for you when you arrive. All that's left to do now is pack your bags and take off. When you do, you take with you my best wishes for a very successful academic and athletic career.

CHAPTER 10

FINDING ALTERNATE ROUTES TO COLLEGE ATHLETICS

Craig Berelli collected his name in headlines from the sports pages like young boys collect baseball cards. On almost any spring day, Craig could plop down a few coins on the corner-store counter, pick up the local news and add another baseball story to his scrapbook. Naturally, it wasn't long before the recruiters came calling.

But eventually Craig had to face the fact that athletic skill alone couldn't carry him into college. The recruiters stopped calling when his SAT scores peaked at 550 and his final GPA hit a low 1.25. Craig didn't meet the NCAA academic eligibility requirements. So in May of his senior year it was obvious that he wasn't going to play for a four-year college. But that didn't mean he had to give up on his goal because Craig knew that the recruiting process doesn't have to end at graduation.

There are many reasons you may find yourself, like Craig, about to graduate high school with no place to go. You may have entered the recruiting game too late or you may have contacted the wrong schools. You may not have the grades to go where you want or you may not have the athletic skill coaches are looking for. Whatever the reason, if you're determined to compete at a four-year college, there are still ways to get there. You can find your way to a four-year college team through a two-year college or a prep school. You can arrive as a walk-on or work your way up through a club team. And if all these attempts fail there's always an intramural team glad to have you.

TWO-YEAR COLLEGES

Lots of athletes start their college careers at two-year colleges. Although the exact number of athletes who transfer into four-year colleges is unknown, it is known that over 50 percent of all students attending college begin at one of America's 1,221 community, technical or junior colleges.

There are a number of reasons you might consider the same route. In the two-year college, which is usually less competitive than the four-year college, athletes can often improve their sport skills and put themselves in a more desirable recruiting position. Two-year colleges also give students some time to adjust to the college curriculum in smaller classes with more individualized attention and without the demands of high-pressure athletics. Also, athletes who don't get the hoped-for athletic scholarship at a four-year college can often earn an athletic scholarship to a two-year college or can afford the average $825 per year tuition at public community colleges; then while saving money and earning college credits, these athletes can sometimes improve their athletic skills and eventually earn the scholarship they want at the four-year school. Two-year colleges are also a desirable option for student-athletes who don't satisfy college or athletic association academic eligibility requirements. Most public junior and community colleges have an open-door admission policy. This means that no specific high school grade point average or test score is required. Frequently a high school diploma or the equivalent is all you need for admission.

The Athletic Program

If you decide to attend a two-year college and want to participate in its athletic program, the recruiting process is very much the same as described throughout this book. You or your coach should contact the college coach and send the same personal and athletic profile used by athletes contacting coaches at four-year colleges. The timing for this contact, however, is often different than recommended in earlier chapters. If you know early in your senior year that you want to attend a two-year school, contact the coach as soon as possible, especially if you'd like an athletic scholarship. Like NCAA schools, many two-year colleges have a limited number of athletic scholarships they can award so the earlier you make your contact, the better your chances of earning a spot on the team and a scholarship. However, because very often student-athletes don't choose a two-year school until all other options are exhausted, late spring and even summer after your senior year are not too late to make your first contact.

If eventual transfer into a four-year college and its athletic program is your goal, be sure to look into the athletic program at the two-year college before you apply. Some two-year colleges don't have any athletic programs; others have only a limited number, and still others offer a comprehensive program in reputable and competitive leagues that are frequently scouted by college coaches. Those colleges that offer intercollegiate sport programs probably belong to an athletic association that can give you all the information you need to make an informed decision.

Athletic Associations

Most two-year colleges in California belong to the California Association of Community Colleges (CACC), which governs the athletic eligibilty rules of its member schools. If you are considering attending a community college in this state be sure to contact the CACC for its regulations. Write to them at: CACC, 2017 "O" Street, Sacramento, California 95814 (916-444-8641).

Outside the state of California, 550 two-year colleges belong to the National Junior College Athletic Association (NJCAA), which governs most junior-college athletics in this country. This association has established rules for the sports of baseball, basketball, bowling, cross country, field hockey, football, golf, gymnastics, ice hockey, lacrosse, marathon, softball, snow skiing, soccer, swimming, tennis, track and field, volleyball and wrestling.

You can participate in these sports as an entering freshman if you meet certain academic requirements outlined in the booklet, *Eligibility Rules of the National Junior College Athletic Association*. These requirements include: (1) Students must be high school graduates, have received a high school equivalency diploma or have been certified as having passed a national test such as the General Education Development Test (GED), or (2) non-high school graduates can establish eligibility for athletic participation by completing one term of college work, passing 12 credits with a 1.75 GPA or higher. This term must be taken after the student's high school class has graduated.

For more information about association rules and regulations you can contact the NJCAA at P.O. Box 7305, Colorado Springs, Colorado 80933 (719-590-9788).

Transfer Rules

The athletic associations of the two-year colleges regulate the rules of sports participation in their member schools, but the athletic associations of the four-year colleges regulate the rules of transfer into their institutions. Before you enroll in a two-year college be sure you understand what criteria you must satisfy to transfer into a four-year college and athletic program. If you wait until you're ready to transfer, you may find that you aren't eligible to play your sport at the college of your choice.

TRANSFER RULES OF THE NATIONAL COLLEGIATE ATHLETIC ASSOCIATION

The transfer rules for student-athletes entering four-year colleges governed by the National Collegiate Athletic Association (NCAA) vary according to the Division the athlete is entering.

DIVISION III TRANSFER RULES

Transfer students who are accepted into a college at any point in their academic career through the normal admissions process are immediately eligible for participation in a Division III sport.

DIVISION II TRANSFER RULES

Student-athletes who transfer from a two-year college into a four-year college are eligible to participate only on the subvarsity level in Division II sports for one full year after transfer unless they meet these eligibility requirements:

- graduate from the two-year college,

OR

- present a minimum of 24 semester or 36 quarter hours of transferable degree credits with a cumulative GPA of 2.000.

Exceptions to the rule: (1) Athletes who were qualifiers out of high school but who were never recruited for a college athletic program and never participated in an intercollegiate sport at a two-year college can transfer to a four-year college and play a Division II sport without meeting the athletic eligibility requirements stated above. (2) Qualifiers who attend a two-year college that does not sponsor their sport or that drops the sport from the athletic program can transfer to a four-year college Division II program without meeting these athletic eligibility requirements.

DIVISION I TRANSFER RULES

Division I schools divide their transfer rules into two groups: those for students who upon high school graduation qualified for NCAA athletic participation, and those for students who were either partial or nonqualifers.

TRANSFER RULES FOR NCAA QUALIFERS

Student-athletes who transfer from a two-year college into a four-year college are not allowed to participate in a Division I sport for one full year unless they meet these eligibility requirements:

- spend two semesters or three quarters at a two-year college (excluding summers)
- complete a minimum of 24 semester hours of transferable degree credits with a cumulative GPA of 2.000

OR

- graduate from a two-year college and complete satisfactorily a minimum of 48 semester or 72 quarter hours of transferable degree credits with a cumulative GPA of 2.000.

Exception to the Rule: Qualifers who attend a two-year college that does not sponsor their sport or which drops the sport from the athletic program can transfer to a four-year college Division I program without meeting the athletic eligibility requirements stated above.

TRANSFER RULES FOR NCAA PARTIAL OR NONQUALIFIERS

Student-athletes who transfer from a two-year college into a four-year college are not eligible to participate in a Division I sport for one full year unless they have graduated from a two-year college and completed satisfactorily a minimum of 48 semester or 72 quarter hours of transferable credits with 2.000 GPA. Partial and non-qualifers cannot be contacted by Division I college recruiters during their first year at a two-year college.

Students who do not meet these transfer eligibility requirements are not eligible for athletic scholarships, regular season competition or practice during the first academic year. If after one year these students satisfy the academic progress requirements of the institution and the athletic conference, they then become eligible for athletic-based financial aid, sport practice and intercollegiate competition.

Obviously, the courses you take and the progress you make during your time at a two-year college directly affect your ability to land on the four-year college team of your choice.

TRANSFER RULES OF THE NATIONAL ASSOCIATION
OF INTERCOLLEGIATE ATHLETICS

The National Association of Intercollegiate Athletics (NAIA) regulates the rules of transfer for its member institutions. To be eligible to participate in one of their athletic programs transfer students must first satisfy the requirements of the institution and/or conference itself. Then they must meet the association's progress rules that govern all athletes. The regulation directly affecting a transfer states that a student who has participated in an intercollegiate contest at the immediately previous four-year institution shall be required to be in residence (sit out) for a period of 16 calendar weeks before being eligible for the sport(s) previously participated in at the previous four-year institution. However, there are several exceptions to this regulation. The faculty athletics representative at any NAIA member institution can explain those exceptions.

If your goal in attending a two-year college is to transfer to a four-year school and participate in athletics, think ahead. Make sure that the courses you take in the junior or community college will be accepted by the college where you intend to transfer. For more information about two-year colleges in general talk to your guidance counselor, call the college directly or write: ERIC Clearinghouse for Junior Colleges, University of California at Los Angeles, 8118 Mathematical Sciences Building, 405 Hilgard Ave., Los Angeles, California 90024; 310-825-3931.

PREP SCHOOLS

Prep schools offer one-year college-preparatory programs. Essentially they offer a fifth year of high school because the grades earned in this additional year become part of the high school transcript.

Prep schools give student-athletes two valuable opportunities: (1) an extra year to grow in athletic skill and maturity (without losing a year of collegiate eligibility), and (2) a chance to improve academic standing to qualify for admission to selective colleges or to satisfy athletic association eligibility requirements.

I asked Jeffrey Cain, College Placement Director at Admiral Farragut Academy, how a prep school can improve students' academic records in just one year when they couldn't do it themselves in the four years before. His response makes a lot of sense.

Prep schools focus solely on a college prep curriculum—no distractions or extras. The classes are small, offer individualized attention and provide an intense academic environment where there's no room for fooling around or wasting time. Prep school teachers often have advanced degrees and have the advantage of working with motivated students. Also, most prep schools employ full-time college placement counselors who personally guide each student through the college selection and application process. Some are military schools, which emphasize the structure and discipline that some students need to accomplish their goals. Under these conditions students certainly can raise their level of academic achievement.

Prep schools are privately owned and operated and so they can be quite expensive, some costing almost $10,000. But many offer need-based scholarships and families like Paula Rivera's consider the cost a down payment on a promising future.

Paula wanted to play basketball at a Division I college. Although several Division I coaches actively recruited her, her plans changed when her SAT scores landed under the 700 combined score required by NCAA eligibility regulations. Paula considered going to a two-year college, but she didn't want to put in the full two years required for Division I transfer and she didn't want to give up those two seasons of Division I eligibility. It was a college recruiter who suggested that Paula go to a prep school where she could raise her SAT scores, practice her sport without forfeiting a year of eligibility and then enroll in a four-year college as if she were coming right out of high school. The prep school option was just what Paula had been looking for.

If you need an additional year to get your grades or your athletic skills up to par, prep schools may be just right for you too. You can locate prep schools through your high school guidance counselor or by consulting the reference book, *Handbook of Private Schools*, which is part of the Sergeants Handbook Series.

WALK-ONS

A walk-on is an athlete who is not invited to play for a college team through the high school recruiting process, but once enrolled in the college asks to try out for the team. As soon as the practice sessions begin, walk-ons should approach the coach and explain their wish to compete on the team. Most often the walk-on will be invited to practice with the team for a few days and this constitutes the "try-out." Walk-ons who make a favorable impression during these practices may be invited to stay on the team.

Frank McLaughlin, Director of Athletics at Fordham University, feels strongly about the importance of walk-ons. "If you don't make it as a recruit," he says, "it's not the end of the line. The success of athletic programs in most schools relies on walk-ons. When I talk with the incoming freshman class at the beginning of each year, I always encourage all students to come out for athletics." Athletic directors around the country echo McLaughlin's feelings, so don't be shy about showing up at practice and asking for a try out. (Some large university football and basketball programs don't allow walk-on athletes because they're financed sufficiently to have their entire team in place before the season begins. But coaches in all other sports encourage enrolled students to try out.)

The walk-on experience of a local baseball player recently made news headlines, which read: "Peters' Perserverance Is Justly Rewarded." Jim Peters was ready to give up on baseball when he went to college. During high school, Peters had received a few letters from local recruiters, but he had not been seriously considered in the recruiting game. The news article explained why: "The designated-hitter rule kept Jim Peters out of the batter's box for most of his high school baseball career." But the article continued, "A little more than a year later, he is a power hitter with a bright college future." During most of his high school career Peters was *DH'd* for, which kept him from compiling impressive statistics or earning local awards or designations. But Peters continued to play in the American Legion leagues and when he arrived at college decided to try out for the sport he loved. "I had nothing to lose," Peters said. "I just decided to do my best and if they wanted to make me part of their team, then they would." And they did. In his freshman year, Peters saw varsity action in the spring and made the most of his at-bats. He went 4-for-7 with a triple and one home run.

Some talented walk-ons even earn athletic scholarships. If you prove yourself and make a significant impact on the team in the first season, you could very well receive athletic-based aid the following year. Peters' advice to high school athletes who aren't recruited says it all: "If you stick it out, you can win out."

CLUB SPORTS

Student-athletes who don't make the college team as a recruit or a walk-on still have opportunities through club sports for athletic participation, exposure and recruitment. Club sports vary from school to school in terms of organization, but generally speaking the format is the same. Club sports utilize college facilities and are open to all interested students. They are financed through member dues and college funding. Student members organize the team, arrange their own schedules and often compete against teams from other schools. Larger colleges may self-select a small group of team members to compete on a more competitive level. Rutgers University, for example, has a swim team whose members are drawn from the swim club. This group is separate from the varsity swim team.

The number of sports offered on the club team level varies among institutions. Some have club teams that provide for the athletic interests of students whose sport isn't sponsored by the college on the varsity level. If, for example, a school doesn't support a varsity ice-hockey program, it will probably sponsor an ice hockey club. Some colleges offer club sports in activities such as karate, frisbee and touch football, which are not varsity sports at all. And many schools offer a comprehensive range of both varsity and club team programs.

Just as large schools may not look for walk-ons to complete their football and basketball rosters, they rarely draw talent from club teams. But in most other sports, the club team offers an excellent opportunity for one last shot at varsity participation. You can use your club sport as a place to practice and improve your skills against college players. If you build up an impressive record, don't wait to be discovered. Just as you would begin the recruiting process in high school, contact the varsity coach and send an updated personal and athletic profile.

Quite often, club team members choose to stay with the club program. Beckey Thomas, for example, joined a club volleyball team hoping to move up to the varsity level eventually. But when the first season ended, Beckey decided that the club team was just what she was looking for. "Our club team has uniforms; we play a full-season schedule, and we compete against an assortment of competitive college teams. The only big difference that I've seen between my club team and the varsity team is the required time and attitude commitment. We don't practice nearly as much as the varsity players and if I don't go to a practice it's no big deal. I've even skipped games without worrying about it when I had to study." Lots of college students find that club teams give them a chance to compete athletically without losing control of their schedule and priorities. So if your goal is simply to compete in your sport, a club team may be the way to go.

INTRAMURAL ATHLETICS

Intramural sports are the most informal athletic programs organized and supervised by college staff members. These teams are open to all interested students (most are coeducational) and they compete against teams made up of other students from the same school. Very often dormitories, fraternities and sororities, and even groups of friends band together to form the intramural teams.

Intramurals are usually offered in a wide-range of sports. They are a fun way to meet people, get some exercise and practice a sport. But they are not a realistic route to varsity participation. If you've come to the end of the recruitment line and still haven't made it to the varsity level, intramurals are the place where you can accept your fate and still enjoy your sport.

If your high school recruiting experience indicates that you may not find your way to the varsity team, you should add the availability of club and intramural teams to your criteria list when choosing a college. If two colleges have similar academic and social and financial characteristics, the club and intramural programs may end up being your deciding factor. For more information about these athletic programs contact the college's Recreational Services Office or the athletic department.

If you have followed the process explained in this book and have found it has helped you in specific ways or fell short in some areas, let me know. My own recruiting efforts continue and your experiences will help me keep up to date on what's happening in college recruiting. Although I can't answer all letters personally, if you'd like to pass along your recruiting experiences drop me a note at this address:

Jack DiSalvo
14 Dawn Place
Wayne, NJ 07470

APPENDIX: SPORTS ASSOCIATIONS

FOR SPECIFIC SPORTS

U.S. BASEBALL FEDERATION
2160 Greenwood Avenue
Trenton, NJ 08609
(609) 586-2381

AMATEUR BASKETBALL ASSOCIATION OF THE UNITED
  STATES
1750 E. Boulder Street
Colorado Springs, CO 80909
(719) 632-7687

YOUNG AMERICAN BOWLING ALLIANCE
5301 S. 76th Street
Greendale, WI 53129
(414) 421-4700

UNITED STATES DIVING, INC.
Pan American Plaza
201 S. Capitol Avenue, Suite 430
Indianapolis, IN 46225
(317) 237-5252

U.S. FENCING ASSOCIATION
1750 E. Boulder Street
Colorado Springs, CO 80909
(719) 578-4511

FIELD HOCKEY ASSOCIATION OF AMERICA (men's)
1750 Boulder Street
Colorado Springs, CO 80909
(719) 578-4587

U.S.A. FIELD HOCKEY ASSOCIATION (women's)
1750 Boulder Street
Colorado Springs, CO 80909
(719) 578-4567

AMERICAN JUNIOR GOLF ASSOCIATION
2415 Steeplechase Lane
Rosewell, GA 30076
(404) 998-4653

UNITED STATES GYMNASTICS FEDERATION
201 S. Capitol Avenue, Suite 300
Indianapolis, IN 46225
(317) 237-5050

U.S.A. AMATEUR HOCKEY ASSOCIATION
Dept. of Coaching/Youth Programs
2997 Broadmoor Valley Road
Colorado Springs, CO 80906
(719) 576-4990

LACROSSE FOUNDATION
John Hopkins University
34th and Charles Streets
Baltimore, MD 21218
(301) 235-6882

UNITED STATES WOMEN'S LACROSSE ASSOCIATION, INC.
45 Maple Avenue
Hamilton, NY 13346
(315) 824-2480

NATIONAL RIFLE ASSOCIATION OF AMERICA
College/Schools Section
1600 Rhode Island Avenue N.W.
Washington, D.C. 20036
(202) 828-6000

NATIONAL INTERCOLLEGIATE RODEO ASSOCIATION
1815 Portland Avenue, Suite 3
Walla Walla, WA 99362
(509) 529-4402

THE UNITED STATES ROWING ASSOCIATION
201 S. Capitol Avenue, Suite 400
Indianapolis, IN 46225
(317) 237-5656

UNITED STATES SKI ASSOCIATION
PO Box 100
Park City, UT 84060
(801) 649-9090

INTERCOLLEGIATE SOCCER ASSOCIATION OF AMERICA
Event Management
1821 Sunny Drive
St. Louis, MO 63112
(314) 349-1967

AMATEUR SOFTBALL ASSOCIATION
2801 N.E. 50th Street
Oklahoma City, OK 73111
(405) 424-5266

NATIONAL INTERSCHOLASTIC SWIMMING COACHES
  ASSOCIATION OF AMERICA
4000 W. Lake Avenue
Glenview, IL 60025
(708) 729-2000

UNITED STATES TENNIS ASSOCIATION
707 Alexander Road
Princeton, NJ 08540
(609) 452-2580

THE ATHLETIC CONGRESS OF THE U.S.A. (track and field)
1 Hoosier Dome, Suite 140
Indianapolis, IN 46225
(317) 261-0500

UNITED STATES VOLLEYBALL ASSOCIATION
3595 E. Fountain Boulevard
Colorado Springs, CO 80910
(719) 597-8333

USA WRESTLING
225 W. Academy Boulevard
Colorado Springs, CO 80910
(719) 597-8333

FOR GENERAL INFORMATION

AMATEUR ATHLETIC UNION OF THE UNITED STATES
  (AAU)
3400 W. 86th Street
PO Box 68207
Indianapolis, IN 46268
(317) 872-2900

NATIONAL ASSOCIATION OF INTERCOLLEGIATE
  ATHLETICS (NAIA)
1221 Baltimore
Kansas City, MO 64105
(816) 842-5050

NATIONAL COLLEGIATE ATHLETIC ASSOCIATION (NCAA)
6201 College Boulevard
Overland Park, KS 66211
(913) 339-1906

NATIONAL JUNIOR COLLEGE ATHLETIC ASSOCIATION
  (NJCAA)
PO Box 7305
Colorado Springs, CO 80933
(719) 590-9788

WOMEN'S SPORTS FOUNDATION
342 Madison Avenue, Suite 728
New York, NY 10173
(212) 972-9170
(Publishes annual *Women's Athletic Scholarship Guide*)

INDEX

A

AAU 5, 13, 17, 153
academic ability 59
academic standards 25–26
  nonqualifier 115–116
  partial qualifier 115–116
  qualifier 115–116
academic suitability 27–29, 128
admissions
  requirements 5
  slots 118
ACT 4, 28, 29, 40, 44, 63, 65, 67, 73
Admiral Farragut Academy 145
admissions officer 83–84, 92
alumni 11, 41
Amateur Athletic Union *See* AAU
Amateur Softball Association 152
American College Test *See* ACT
American College Testing Program 120
American Junior Golf Association 151
American Legion Baseball 17
AMVETS 122
applications
  appearance 92
  common form 95
  essay 95
  guidance counselor section 98–99
  student section 94
  teacher recommendation 99–100
  timing 102–104
Arizona State 29, 37
Assumption College 117
athletic associations 62 *See also* NCAA, NAIA
Athletic Congress of the U.S.A. 153
athletic placement services 55–57
athletic scholarships
  financial aid 116–117
  pros and cons of 109–112
  NAIA 117–118
  NCAA 112–117
  questionnaires 119

B

Babe Ruth League 17
badminton 12
Barron's Profiles of American Colleges 32
baseball 51, 63, 73, 114, 118
basketball 51, 63, 68, 73, 114, 115, 118, 135
Bentley College 117
Bird, Larry 24, 41
blue chip athletes 36, 37
  eligibility of 4
boosters 71–72

Boras, Scott 69
Boston University 28, 77
Brooklyn College 117
Brown University 103, 113 *See also* Ivy League Schools
Bucknell University 96, 117
Burger King Crew Member Scholarship 122

C

CACC *See* California Association of Community Colleges
Cain, Jeffrey 145
California Association of Community Colleges 140–141
camps 11, 14–16, 17
  cost 21
  Cronauer's B/C All–Star 15
  evaluation of 19–22
  Garfinkel's Five–Star 15
  Krider's All American 15
campus visits
  admissions officer and 83–84
  college coach and 81
  faculty members and 84–85
  junior year 79–80
  parents and 88
  preparation for 78–79
  rules 86–88
  senior year 80–81
  student/athletes and 85–86
  timing of 79–81
Canisius College 117
Center for Sports and Society 37
Central Connecticut State 117
clinics 11
club sports 147–148
coaches 18
  recruiting rules for 71
  skill evaluation 8, 10
Colgate University 117

College Athletic Placement Service (CAPS) 56
College Scholarship Service 120
college selection
  academic suitability 27–29
  athletic program 33–35
  cost 30
  location 30–32
  size 32–33
College of William and Mary 118
Columbia University 32, 103, 113 *See also* Ivy League schools
Connie Mack league 17
Cornell University 77, 83, 103, 113 *See also* Ivy League schools
Council of Ivy Group Presidents 113
crew 12, 51
cross country 12, 73, 114, 115, 118
C.W. Post College 117

D

Dartmouth College 103, 113 *See also* Ivy League schools
Directory of College Athletics 50
diving 73, 118
Drive: The Story of My Life 24
Duquesne College 117

E

early action 103
early decision 102–103
East Coast Athletic Conference 117
Eastern Invitational Tournament 13
Educational Testing Service 100

ERIC Clearinghouse for Junior Colleges 144

F

faculty athletics representatives 76
Family Educational Rights and Privacy Act 100
fencing 12, 51, 63, 114, 115
field hockey 12, 17, 51, 56, 63, 115
Field Hockey Association 151
financial aid 120–126
  athletic scholarships and 116–117
  checklist 125
  federal and state aid 121–122
  institutional aid 120
  miscellaneous sources for 124
Financial Aid Form 120
Financial Aid Statement 120
football 51, 63, 68, 73, 114, 118, 135
Fordham University 130, 146
frisbee 12

G

Gannon College 117
Georgetown University 29
Gibbons, Bob 22
GIS Guide to Four-Year Colleges 40
goals 3, 11
  athletic 35–39
  focusing on 6
  planning 4–6
  realistic 8
Goldbrenner, Sharon 56
golf 12, 51, 63, 73, 114, 115, 118
Graphic Arts Technical Foundation Program 122

guidance counselor 8, 28, 40, 62, 93, 98–99, 121
Guidance Information System 40
gymnastics 12, 51, 63, 114, 115

H

Harvard University 103, 113, 130
  See also Ivy League schools
Hilliard, Richard 61
Hofstra University 28
Holy Cross College 117
Horford, Tito 68

I

ice hockey 12, 51, 63, 68, 114
Indiana University 24, 29, 130
Intercollegiate Soccer Association of America 152
intramural athletics 148–149
Iona College 117
Ivy League schools 103, 113, 136

J

James Madison University 13
Jayhawks 17
Johns Hopkins University 96

K

Keller, Steve 22
King's College 96

L

lacrosse 12, 17, 51, 56, 63, 68, 114, 115
Lacrosse Foundation 151
Lafayette College 77, 117
LA Gear 15

leagues 16–17
  cost of 21
  evaluation of 19–22
Lehigh University 117
Lenoir–Rhyne College 87–88

M

Manhattan College 77, 88
Marist College 117
Massachusetts Institute of Technology (MIT) 103
McLaughlin, Frank 130, 146
Mercyhurst College 117
Michigan State University 28, 37, 58
MidAtlantic Sporting News 22
Midyear Report 106
multisport athletes 6, 7

N

NAIA 26, 34, 62, 72, 153
  amateur status 74–75
  athletic scholarships 117
  campus visit regulations 87–88
  eligibility requirements 4, 73
  evaluation periods 74
  recruiting regulations 73–74
  rules and regulations 61
  scholarships 117–118
  transfer rules 144
  tryouts 74
National Ambucs Scholarship Program 122
National Association of College Admission Counselors 107
National Athletic Intercollegiate Association *See* NAIA
National Basketball Association 37
National Collegiate Athletic Association *See* NCAA
National Directory of College Athletics 12

National Intercollegiate Rodeo Association 152
National Interscholastic Swimming Coaches 152
National Junior College Athletic Association 62, 141, 154
National Letter of Intent 61, 67, 70, 134–137
  signing periods 135
National Rifle Association of America 152
NCAA 10, 26, 29, 32, 41, 153
  amateur status 69–70
  Bylaw 14.3 63, 115
  camps and 16
  campus visit regulations 86–87
  contact periods 51, 66–68
  divisions 34
  eligibility regulations 4, 63
  evaluation periods 67–68
  recruiting regulations 66–68
  rules and regulations 58–59, 62–72
  scholarships 112–117
  transfer rules 142–143
  tryouts 68
NCAA Guide for the College-Bound Student-Athlete 87
Nike camps 15, 22
NJCAA *See* National Junior College Athletic Association
NLI *See* National Letter of Intent
nonscholarship schools 117
North Carolina State 29
North Wesleyan College 29
Notre Dame 28, 130

O

off season 7
  leagues and tournaments 16, 21
Ohio State 131

Orleans, Jeffrey 113
Orschiedt, Peter 77, 83

P

Pace College 117
parachuting 12
Pell Grants 121
Perkins Loans 121
Peterson's Four-Year Colleges 40
placement services
  counselors 11
PLUS loans 122
polo 12
Preliminary Scholastic Aptitude Test *See* PSAT
prep schools 144–145
pressure
  in college athletics 2, 3
Princeton University 28, 103, 113
  See also Ivy League schools
Proposition 48 63
PSAT 28, 67

Q

qualifiers 115–116
  See also academic standards
questions
  for admissions officers 84
  for coaches 82
  for faculty 85
  for student-athletes 86

R

recommendations
  athletic 47
  teacher 99–100
recruiters
  unofficial 70–72, 75
recruiting services 20

resume
  academic information 44–45
  athletic profile 45–46
  cover letter 48–49
  news clippings 47
  recommendations 47–48
Rhoads, Robert 75
rifle 63, 114
rodeo 12
rolling admissions 104

S

Sacred Heart College 117
SAT 4, 26, 29, 40, 44, 63, 64, 65, 67, 73
scholarship
  NCAA and NAIA 36
  services 123
Scholastic Aptitude Test *See* SAT
School Report 98
scouting reports 20
scouts 11
Seaver, Tom 43
senior slide 104, 106–107
SEOG *See* Supplemental Educational Opportunity Grants
Serra, Bill 56
Siena College 117
Skiing 12, 63, 114, 115
skill
  evaluation 8
  second opinion on 10–11
soccer 12, 17, 51, 68, 73, 114, 115, 118, 135
softball 51, 63, 73, 115, 118
Sports Factory, The 43
Sports Illustrated 15, 16, 22, 131
squash 12, 51
St. Francis College (PA) 117
St. John's College 117
St. Peter's College 117

Stafford Loans 121

Stan Musial League 17

Statement of Students' Rights and Responsibilities in the College Admission Process 107

Supplemental Educational Opportunity Grants (SEOG) 121

Swarthmore College 118

swimming 12, 17, 51, 63, 73, 114, 115, 118

T

tagging 118

Taylor, Brien 69, 74

teacher recommendations 99–100

tennis 12, 51, 73, 114, 115, 118

tournaments 16–17

cost of 21

evaluation of 19–22

track and field 12, 51, 63, 118

transcript 98

Trenton State 56

Tufts University 94

two-year colleges 139–144

athletic associations of 140–141

transfer rules 141–144

U

United States Diving, Inc. 151

United States Fencing Association 151

United States Gymnastic Federation 151

United States Rowing Association 152

United States Ski Association 152

United States Tennis Association 153

United States Volleyball Association 153

United States Women's Lacrosse Association, Inc. 152

University of Houston 68

University of Kentucky 59

University of Minnesota 58

University of Nevada-Las Vegas 37

University of North Carolina-Charlotte 32

University of Pennsylvania 103, 113 *See also* Ivy League schools

University of Rhode Island 32

University of Southern California 43

University of Texas-Dallas 29

University of Vermont 77

U.S.A. Amateur Hockey Association 151

U.S.A. Field Hockey Association 151

U.S.A. Wrestling 153

U.S. Service Academies 28, 136

USTA (United States Tennis Association) 17

V

video tapes 53–55

volleyball 12, 17, 51, 63, 73, 114, 115, 118

W

Wagner College 117

walk-on 146–147

water polo 63, 114

weight training 7

Winfield, A Player's Life 1
Winfield, Dave 1, 12
Woman's Sports Foundation 154
Worksheets
  #1 38
  #2 42
  #3 105
  #4 130

wrestling 12, 17, 51, 63, 68, 73, 114, 118

Y

Yale University 103, 113 *See also* Ivy League schools
Yankees 69, 74